The Expert Ex... ...fit-Producing Trade Sh... ...orate Events

THE PLATINUM RULE®

for

TRADE SHOW MASTERY

*"Do Unto Others as **They** Would Have You Do Unto Them"*

DR. TONY ALESSANDRA
STEVE UNDERATION, CTSM
SCOTT MICHAEL ZIMMERMAN

✚ **PLATINUM RULE PRESS**

New York

THE PLATINUM RULE *for* TRADE SHOW MASTERY

Tony Alessandra, Ph.D.
Steve Underation, Certified Trade Show Marketer
Scott Michael Zimmerman
© 2008 Alessandra, Underation, Zimmerman

ISBN: 978-1-60037-329-9 (Paperback)

Published by:

✛ PLATINUM RULE PRESS

an imprint of

Morgan James Publishing, LLC

1225 Franklin Ave. Ste 325

Garden City, NY 11530-1693

Toll Free 800-485-4943

www.MorganJamesPublishing.com

Interior Design by:
Bonnie Bushman
bbushman@bresnan.net

DEDICATIONS

From Tony Alessandra: *I dedicate this book to my mother - Margaret Alessandra - who instilled in me the desire and drive to succeed and excel.*

From Steve Underation: *This book is dedicated to my Christian brother Scott "Socrates" Zimmerman.*

For your vision to build The Cyrano System to help sales and marketing professionals spend less time on the road and more time with their families. Your great gift to all of us "road warriors."

For your encouragement, contribution, and quarterbacking to make sure this book made it into print.

For the unselfish giving of your Light, time, talent, and treasure to change the lives and lift the careers of others. This is the true meaning of how to win friends and influence people. For these blessings and many others, I thank you.

Dale Carnegie would be very proud of you, my friend.

From Scott Zimmerman: *Sweet P, my one and only; thank you for sharing your life with me. Steve, my brother in Christ, thank you for "getting" my marketing ideas, thank you for being my friend, but most of all I'm grateful for your support along my faith journey! Glenn, thank you for your years of loyal service, your incredible talents and for being a truly wonderful friend. Tony, thank you for letting me share in your greatest discovery: The Platinum Rule, and for your wisdom, guidance and mentorship. Jim Cathcart: Thanks again for returning my call, listening to my story and introducing me to Tony.*

INSIDE THIS BOOK

V

TRADE SHOWS:

SECTION II — INSIDERS SECRETS: WINNING WITH ADVANCED PLATINUM RULE STRATEGIES

THE AUTOBAHN OR THE SCENIC TOUR:

THE BANQUET OR THE BANK VAULT:

DIRECTORS...

SECTION III — THE TRADE SHOW MASTERY SYSTEM USING PLATINUM RULES 65

BRIGHT LIGHTS, BIG CITY:
Thriving Trade Shows are a Three-Act Play 66

ACT ONE, PRE-SHOW:
Draw Bull's-eyes, Don't Herd Cats 66

ACT TWO, AT-SHOW:
Be the Pincushion, Not the Needle in the Haystack 68

ACT THREE, POST-SHOW:
Where Are the Leads? 69

THE BIG AUDITION:
Leverage Pre-Show Success with Platinum Planning 70

THE CURTAIN RISES:
Use Platinum Guidelines to Reduce Show Stress 82

SECTION IV — WINNING WITH PLATINUM RULES BEYOND THE EXHIBIT HALL.......... 135

THE END OF THIS BOOK, A NEW BEGINNING 201

ABOUT THE AUTHORS 209

Contributors and Resources 215

FROM THE AUTHORS

Welcome to an exciting new chapter in The Platinum Rule book series: *The Platinum Rule for Trade Show Mastery*. This book is written as the first specific application of the original book _The Platinum Rule_ to the trade show and event marketplace. The extension of The Platinum Rule into this arena is timely because many exhibitors endure tremendous pressure by top management to produce new customers, increase sales, and document a measurable return on show investment, without a roadmap or system to get there.

Smart exhibitors understand that no matter how large or spectacular their booth presence may be, people still buy from individual people they like and trust. Whether your industry is Business-to-Business, or Business-to-Consumer, the reality is that all market sales are done P-to-P, or Person-to-Person. Therefore, effective companies make their entire trade show and event an "experience" while targeting people on an individual level, considering specific behavioral types.

This book also transfers the basic tenets of _The Platinum Rule for Sales Mastery_ and _The Platinum Rule for Personal Marketing Mastery_ directly into the trade show and event marketplace. Since trade shows and events have sales and marketing as two of their three major components (exhibit design and building is the third), you will benefit by reading these two books after you have read this one. We hope that you have read *The Platinum Rule* by now to fully understand "why" The Platinum Rule should become the standard way of doing business for you and your company.

We also know that readers like to graze through a book, no longer having unlimited blocks of time to dedicate to reading chapters in a sitting. We respect your busy schedule and give you a book that you can read in bite-sized chunks on a plane, in an airport, at your hotel, or wherever your travels may take you. Your lifestyle is respected in this book, and we give you the information in a way that allows you to pick up the book and put it down during your busy day without losing your train of thought.

At the same time, this book is not meant to be the definitive encyclopedia to trade shows and events. We intentionally left out many of the common exhibit industry statistics and trade show methodology found in traditional trade show books.

Instead, this book will give you the best ways to identify, capture, qualify, cultivate, and nurture highly qualified prospects. Then we will show you how to convert these highly qualified prospects into customers. Many of these customers will consistently buy from you, pay their bills, and go out of their way to be apostles who spread your good news to others.

It is our goal to help you distinguish yourself personally and memorably to the people you meet.

You are distinguished in the minds of your prospects and customers when you are personable, helpful and therefore different from your competition. We want you to learn how to help other people be comfortable with you, and thereby trust you. When a prospect or customer trusts you, they will want to work with you and buy from you.

Therefore, apply the information in this book to yourself first, and learn how you operate and how others see you. Then, know why others react to you the way they do based on your normal behavior style. Then take what you know about yourself and others and integrate Platinum Rule behavior in your trade shows and events. When you do, other people will respond more favorably to you and your messages. When they do, you are well on your way to distinguishing yourself from your competition and making your trade shows and events an investment and not an expense.

Tony Alessandra, PhD

Steve Underation, Certified Trade Show Marketer

Scott Michael Zimmerman

THE FORGOTTEN TRUTH EVERY EXHIBITOR MUST KNOW

The Platinum Rule is about knowing your own natural behavioral style first, then seeing the natural behaviors of others and adapting your natural behavior to their natural behavior. *"Do unto others as they would like to be done unto."* Serve others in their comfort zone first, yours second. The reward is that trade shows, like life, are about serving the needs of the other person, knowing that when you do, your needs will be served in return.

Unfortunately, many trade show workers and exhibitors do not see the necessity of serving the other person, especially during the course of a show. They focus on their own discomforts and problems, spend a lot of time complaining, deliver less-than-adequate hospitality to their "guests," and as a result miss out on the opportunity to make a positive difference for their prospects and customers. That is why we begin this book with the following story to remind all of us our obligation to keep the other person's needs constantly before us, and respect their situation and needs at all times.

Steve Miller is an expert trade show marketer with 25 plus years of experience. Before starting his company, The Adventure, LLC, he learned his lessons in the trade show industry from the floor, in the "school of hard knocks." As his toughest lesson, Steve tells about an experience he had early in his sales career at the Consumer Electronics Show in Las Vegas. CES is one of the largest trade shows in the world with an attendance of well over 100,000 and over a thousand exhibiting companies. Steve relates his experience this way;

One afternoon, I was in our small booth when a woman named Edith Goldman walked in. Edith was one of my very best customers. She had buying authority in the millions of dollars, so she was very important to my company and me. I spent a few minutes taking Edith through the booth, showing her our products, just as I did with every other visitor. After a few minutes, she said, "You don't want to be here, do you?"

Caught off guard, I sort of stammered my response and said, "Of course I want to be here." She held up her hand and said, "No, you really don't want to be here at this trade show, do you?" I said something along the lines of "Well, it's a big trade show and we have to be here."

Edith paused and said, "Look Steve, I'm not trying to make you feel bad, but I just feel like I need to tell you something.

"Yesterday morning, I was in my apartment in New York City. I packed everything for my trip to Las Vegas, went downstairs, got in a line to grab a taxicab to the airport. I stood in a slow-moving line to get my boarding pass. Then I went to the gate and stood in another line to get on the airplane. While I was on the airplane, I sat in a very narrow seat next to people that I don't even know, eating airplane toy food.

"I landed in Las Vegas, and went to the baggage claim where I waited for my bag. Then, I went and stood in another long, slow-moving line to get a taxi to my hotel. When I got to my hotel, I stood in another line to get checked into my room. I then went to the hotel restaurant and had a lonely dinner by myself, eating hotel quality food. I went to my room and got a restless night's sleep on a bed that a thousand other people had slept on before.

"I got up this morning, went to breakfast by myself in the hotel, and went out and stood in line at the hotel for the bus that would bring me to the convention center. The bus dropped me off and I went in to the convention center and stood in a line to get my badge. Then I waited at the doors for the show to open. Since it opened, I have walked up and down several miles of aisles trying to talk to exhibitors who really don't want to be here."

I was a bit surprised by this story, and I told Edith that I really did not know what she had meant.

"Do you think that I have nothing better to do with my time?" she said. "You see all of those other buyers, walking miles up and down the aisles? You think that they have nothing better to do with their time? The fact is Steve; most exhibitors don't want to be here. They see this trade show as a necessary evil, and many more see it as a nuisance. But buyers like me DO want to be here! So can you imagine HOW MUCH MORE BUSINESS you would have if all you did was just ACT like you WANT to be here?"

I was of course both humbled and educated at the same time. I thanked Edith for her honesty, finished our time together with greater enthusiasm, and spent the rest of the show treating each and every buyer as the valued guest to my booth that they were.

Edith's story to me was the epiphany that I needed to wake me up to the true value of trade shows, and to the situation, sacrifice, and needs of the people visiting my booth. As a result, I have been a student of trade shows ever since, and have committed my efforts to make trade shows a positive experience for the exhibitor and attendee.

Does this story sound like you? Are you either an unmotivated and annoyed exhibitor, or a disappointed and frustrated buyer? Do you verbally and emotionally disconnect between yourself and the people you meet on the other side of the booth?

We are here to use Steve's experience to show you a better way as both exhibitor and attendee, and make the exhibit experience fun, effective, and profitable. If you are tired of the same old drudgery of "doing" a trade show and want to breathe new life into your show experience, then we encourage you to read on to the next section to learn new understandings about yourself.

THE PLATINUM RULE FOR YOU

One size trade show Sales and Marketing does not fit everyone, especially not in today's hyper competitive, multi-media blitz marketplace. Instead, truly effective trade show sales and marketing is tailored like a good suit to fit only the individual person. The tailor bases the fit on the person's true needs, and makes sure the suit is delivered and worn with a personalized approach.

The personalized approach is what makes The Platinum Rule incredibly effective. It shows you how to consistently and easily adapt to every person you meet on a one-to-one basis, thereby building trust, reducing interpersonal tension, and opening the door to new business opportunities.

You can make The Platinum Rule work regardless of how you normally behave. Your ability to develop and use behaviors not necessarily your own natural style for the benefit of the relationship is a called "behavioral adaptability." This type of flexibility is something applied more to you (to your patterns, attitudes and habits) than to others. Behavioral adaptability involves making intentional adjustments to your methods of communicating and behaving, based on the particular needs of the other person. These intentional adjustments are always made based on the behavior exhibited by the other person at that particular moment in time.

Behavioral adaptability is the key to successfully communicating your ideas to people of every style. As you continue to develop more adaptability, you will more effectively interact with each person in the way he or she likes to communicate. Effective communication helps the other person learn, build relationships, transact business, and make purchases.

Adapting your behavioral style is a big change, and big changes take time!

Here is a simple test. Move an appliance you use every day (toaster, coffee maker, electric razor, etc.) before going to bed. Quite likely, when you wake up in the morning and go to make toast, brew coffee or shave, you will automatically go to where the appliance **used to be** as opposed to its new location. The point we are making is that old habits are hard to break, but breaking bad habits is absolutely worth the effort!

It's not easy to break the old habit of "selling the way you buy." You need to learn to reach out to other people based on *their* style, their comfort zone. This means learning to alter your approach, strategies and techniques to fit four uniquely different buying styles.

To date, we guess you have been interacting with other people in a way that "works" for you. Feedback from your parents, siblings, relatives, teachers and friends shaped the way you relate yourself to others. To be able to change your usual behavior patterns you will require practice and focus to "unlearn" the ways you normally relate to other people. The practice and focus will sharpen your interpersonal skills and help you develop better reactions to all types of situations and all types of people.

Understanding your natural behavioral style and learning to recognize another person's style is the first step to trade show mastery.

But unless you are willing to recognize your style, understand the style of the other person, and use the knowledge of The Platinum Rule to adapt both, you have gained nothing from this information. Therefore, the basic platform of the information in this book will teach you how to make small adjustments in your approach to others to reduce tension, build trust, and inevitably convert more of your qualified trade show leads into lifetime, loyal customers.

TYPICAL TRADE SHOW
SELLING MISTAKES

To show you a pre-Platinum Rule scenario, we tell the story of John, a Sales Representative you might meet in booths on the show floor. John is a Sales Representative for a major stamping press manufacturer, working his first trade show. John is excited; he loves people, and grew up with a father who was a press operator. He is confident that he can sell presses and make lots of money. For years, his friends always said John had the "gift of gab" and he was eager to start selling. Walk with John through his show experience to see if the story represents your company today. His first day experience is as follows:

"Old School" Salesmanship: The "Sizzle versus Steak" Dilemma

A man in his early 40s enters the booth and approaches a 50-ton press. John walks up, introduces himself and starts telling the prospect about the press. He remembers a booth sales course comment about how people "buy the sizzle not the steak," so he emphasizes the press's sleek European design, how fast it runs, and how impressive it will look sitting in the prospect's machine shop.

The prospect flips through some papers he brought in with him. He quietly asks John if the press has a process monitor for part quality and safety, and if he has any documentation about the reliability of previous models. John assures him that the press has a process monitor and tells him that a press like this will "run circles around his other presses." He enthusiastically mentions that a major supplier to "The Big Three" just bought the very same model.

The prospect asks about typical production efficiency and John tells him that it "really cranks out the parts," and suggests how happy his operators will be to run the new touch screen controller on the press. The prospect folds his papers, thanks John for his time and leaves... declining to take the brochure sheet and business card John offers him.

John knows that the brief conversation with the prospect didn't go very well, but he's not sure why. He asks his sales manager what went wrong. The manager tells John that maybe the prospect needed more information about safety and value; this is a major purchase and people like to know exactly what they are buying and if it is OSHA approved.

If at First You Don't Succeed...

Two young engineers walk over and look at the same press. John introduces himself and tells them about how well the press is built and carefully describes all the safety features. He assures them that this is a very efficient model, the lowest set-up times for its class. Then one asks about its parts-per-minute rating and the other remarks that it looks kind of "light-duty." John rattles off the torque and tonnage ratings and tells them that "European transfer presses" are the latest rage. They tell John they were "just looking" and thank him as they leave.

John sits down, scratches his head and wonders if he has gotten himself into the wrong field. He wonders how he's going to pay his bills.

What did John do wrong? A **Platinum Rule** advisor would say, "Almost everything." He tried to sell something before he knew the prospect's behavior style and what they really wanted. He didn't ask questions, observe their behaviors and pace, or find out the criteria each customer was using to make their purchasing decisions.

We believe that John made two major errors:

One: John didn't understand his own selling style, nor how to **adapt** to the needs of each prospect. He tried to fit each prospect into a rigid sales mold rather than fitting the sales style he used to the prospect's needs.

Two: John didn't understand the basic **process** of booth sales; how to gather as much qualifying information about the prospect to jump-start the all-important follow-up process. In other words, he talked when he should have listened.

While John might seem like an extreme example, his mistakes aren't that much different from those made every day in trade show booths across the world – new and experienced – in every sales field. The *Platinum Rule for Trade Show Mastery* shows how to match the right product or service to a prospect's needs, matching the prospect's buying pace to the sales pace, and matching your natural behavioral style to the natural style of every prospect and customer. The ability to adapt your style to your prospect and customers' styles helps you build rapport faster and develop strong relationships easier.

HOW TO BEND "THE RULES"
IN YOUR FAVOR

To contrast The Platinum Rule, we must first take a look at "The Golden Rule." If you remember, the Golden Rule is *"Do unto others as **You** would have **Them** do unto You."* The Golden Rule is still a great rule to live by. We believe in it 110%, especially when it comes to honesty, values, ethics and having consideration for the needs of others.

However, when it comes to interpersonal communication, the Golden Rule can backfire because others may not wish to be treated the same way you like to being treated. That's why we advocate that you "bend the rules" by **adopting** the values and ethics of The Golden Rule, and **adapting** your behaviors to others by using The Platinum Rule.

The Platinum Rule came to be when Tony Alessandra moved from New York City to San Diego during the beginnings of his career as a speaker and consultant. Tony soon realized that people on the opposite coasts and everywhere in between are diverse and need to be treated differently. No longer would his natural fast-paced, hard-driving New York City behavioral style work with the laid-back style of Southern California. He disconnected with others by the way he delivered his messages, even though the content was right. The proverbial "swing and a miss!"

To raise his batting average with others, he realized the need for change on his end, and he made the decision to change his approach to match the style of the other person. It worked! All of a sudden people responded to him in a positive light, and he was able to make the personal and professional connections he wanted. It was during this period of his personal and professional growth that he developed the system and coined the phrase, "The Platinum Rule," which states:

*"Do unto others as **They** would have **You** do unto **Them**."*

(Notice the difference..."you" becomes "they")

The Platinum Rule lets you learn and understand the behaviors of others and interact with them in a style that is best for THEM, not just for you. The benefits are that you adapt to the other person while retaining your own identity. The four outcomes from practice of The Platinum Rule are that you can:

1. Lead others in the way they like to follow

2. Speak with them in the way they like to listen

3. Help them learn at their pace, not yours

4. Accelerate their comfort level with you

When you understand your own style and how it differs from the styles of others, you can adapt your approach to stay "on the same wavelength" with them. Your ideas do not have to change, but you can change the way you present your ideas. We call this adaptability.

Consider this: there are four behavioral styles and you have *one* of them. If you sell to all your customers based on the way you like to buy, you are only connecting with those who share your style. What this suggests is that you are not connecting with the three other styles, thereby limiting your full potential to reach a greater audience.

Getting along with others is the universal key to success. In fact, studies have shown that the ability to build rapport with others is the one thing all highly successful people have in common. Mastery of The Platinum Rule is the key to opening the door to successful relationships in all areas of your life... beyond a successful career in trade shows and events.

If you have never taken an accurate test to help you understand your own behavioral style, you should visit http://assessments. platinumrulegroup.com/assessment.asp and answer the questions. Understanding your own strengths and weaknesses is the first step toward increased self-awareness. Heightened self-awareness of your own natural behaviors, and more importantly how they relate to others, will forever change your approach to planning and conducting trade shows and events.

The Platinum Rule for Trade Show Mastery is different from any approach used by trade show marketers. *The Platinum Rule for Trade Show Mastery* is not relationship or personal selling. What we teach you to do in this book is learn one of the most reliable methods for identifying the Behavioral Style of your prospects and customers. Then, when you know their style, you can relate to them the way they like, not the way you want. Give those who pay your salary with their purchases your greatest respect and consideration.

Mastery and application of The Platinum Rule in trade shows and events will lead you to stronger customer relationships, broad-based customer loyalty, and measurable increases in overall sales; all from the trust and comfort you built by considering the needs of your customers first.

SECTION I

THE PLATINUM RULE
QUICK START GUIDE TO
TRADE SHOW MASTERY

S ection One is written for those of you who want to get started on things immediately. Therefore, to get you started as quickly as possible on the road to understanding and using The Platinum Rule in your exhibit and event programs, we created this section.

The Quick Start Guide is a brief overview of the key points you need to know about The Platinum Rule, and begins the process of connecting with the trade show and event marketplace.

After you move through the Quick Start section, you will be ready for the more advanced Platinum Rule strategies, detailed and illustrated in **Section Two:** *The Insiders Guide to Advanced Platinum Rule Strategies.*

YOU ARE HOW YOU ACT:

The Four Behavioral Styles Of Your Prospects And Customers

For some of you, the "four styles" model of human behavior is a new concept. However, many of you have probably run across this concept on more than one occasion. "Behavioral styles," "personality types" and "temperament types" are not new, and they all have validity.

People have been fascinated with studying behavioral styles for thousands of years. Nevertheless, a common thread throughout the centuries is the groupings of human behavior... in four categories. In the context of "The Platinum Rule," the categories are as follows: **the Director, Socializer, Thinker and Relater.**

Knowing your primary style is the first step in the journey to trade show mastery. When you know your style, you will be able to recognize and adapt your style to the people you meet. So read on and see how you fit in the four categories, and then see if you can recognize the style of the people that make the biggest difference in your bottom line.

WHO AM I, WHO ARE THEY?

Quickly Read Your Prospect's Style

We suggest you take the online Platinum Rule Assessment at: http:// assessments.platinumrulegroup.com/assessment.asp. This assessment gives you a head start to the next section and a quick way to identify your style (and the styles of others). In knowing your own style, you are well on your way to having better relationships with people at work, socially and at home.

As you seek to know your style – and that of others – bear in mind that people are not simple creatures; they can be infinitely complex. Every person possesses each of the styles to some degree; so expect to find shades of gray... not black and white. However, people do have one dominant style raising above the other three that gives them their uniqueness. Yes, there are instances where a person may be direct in one setting (work) but indirect when at home; they may be open with their significant other, but guarded with co-workers. So, always deal with the person in the behavior that they are demonstrating at the particular moment in time you are interacting with them.

Before you learn how to "read" the behavioral styles of others, identify your own style. On the following page, you will find a chart of Indirect and Direct behaviors. Read each description of behaviors and check the one that *most closely* describes your behavior. For example, do you tend to "avoid risks" <u>or</u> "take risks?" Check the one that most describes your behavior. Remember, one is not "better" than the other; this is simply a way to begin developing the skill of reading the behavioral style of yourself and others.

Check here if this behavior sounds most like you	"Indirect Behaviors"	or	"Direct Behaviors"	Check here if this behavior sounds most like you
	I tend to be slower paced.	or	I tend to be faster paced.	
	I tend to listen more than talk.	or	I tend to talk more than listen.	
	I am reluctant to directly express my opinions.	or	I find it easy to directly express my opinions.	
	I usually react slowly when faced with new situations or decisions.	or	I usually react quickly when faced with new situations or decisions.	

Check here if this behavior sounds most like you	"Indirect Behaviors"	or	"Direct Behaviors"	Check here if this behavior sounds most like you
	I make decisions after all the facts are available.	or	I make decisions whether or not all the facts are available.	
	I come across as less assertive than others.	or	I come across as more assertive than others.	
	I tend to "bite my tongue" when I don't agree with someone.	or	I tend to "speak my mind" when I don't agree with someone.	
	I get frustrated when things move too quickly.	or	I get impatient when things move too slowly.	
	I generally avoid conflict.	or	I do not avoid conflict.	
	Total "Indirect" checkmarks		**Total "Direct" checkmarks**	

First, having checked the items that most describe you, are you more Indirect or more Direct?

Next, determining whether you express yourself in a more "open" or "guarded" manner will enable you to pinpoint your behavioral style (and that of other people).

We best demonstrate the process of reading the style of a customer through the example of a salesperson preparing for a customer call. Remember, each new encounter, whether in person or over the phone, should begin with you seeking answers to the two basic questions that will help you get a sense of the other person's behavioral style. These answers shape how you should adapt to the style of that individual from that point forward to increase rapport and improve your probability of making a sale. The two key questions you should try to answer as quickly as possible are:

1.	Is this person more Direct or more Indirect?

2.	Is this person more Open or more Guarded?

The ability to determine Guarded/Open and Direct/Indirect is key to the relationship you build or credibility you earn with your customer or prospect. There are other clues you may observe to determine behavioral style, and these are related to their environment. Look for environmental clues that may further confirm your conclusion.

It's Easy:

Simple Techniques to Identify Your Customer Behavior Styles

Here are two simple techniques that will get you well on your way to quickly and accurately reading the behavioral styles of others. Your goal is to determine whether each individual is more direct or indirect and more open or guarded. In doing so, you can quickly determine if each and every customer is a Director, Relater, Socializer or Thinker.

Again, the two "dimensions" that help us determine another person's style are:

1.	How "Direct" or "Indirect" their behaviors are

2.	How "Open" or "Guarded" they are in revealing private thoughts

When you correctly determine the other person's natural style, you are well on your way to a better relationship. This way, you can quickly use the first minute of sometimes-awkward time when you speak with a buyer or attendee to determine your best approach to adapt to their behavioral style.

If nothing more, you can use your understanding of the other person's behavioral style to help improve your answer the age-old trade show question: "So, what does your company do?" Base your answer on the most likely outcome your prospect would need to hear, given entirely with regard to their observed behavioral style.

Now that you have a quick start review of The Platinum Rule, let's take a quick look at trade show marketing as currently practiced by many exhibit professionals.

Are Your Trade Shows Strategy or Tradition?

Your company should make the decision if trade shows and events are to be used as a strategic part of your marketing, or as a necessary evil that you do because you "have to."

Many companies do not realize the power of using trade shows and events as a means to concentrate their value propositions to current and past customers, targeted prospects, and new opportunities.

Typical reasons stated for exhibiting are:

1.   Our competitors are there

2.   People would spread bad rumors if we were not there

3.   We always do it

4.   We don't know why

The truth of the matter is that if you do not make the decision to use trade shows and events as a strategic part of your marketing, you are wasting valuable dollars of your budget that could contribute to your bottom line. Merely attending trade shows for the above reasons has more to do with a lack of focus and purpose in how you spend your marketing dollars.

What Do You Spend and Why?

How much is each trade show lead worth to your company? Have you ever put a dollar figure on each lead, based on the cost to attend the show and the amount of leads you qualify? Would it make a difference in how your company treats trade show leads if you knew that the cost of generating each lead was $100, $500, $1,000 or more per lead?

- If each lead costs you money to generate, what are some of the problems you face after a trade show to make them pay for you?

Direct Marketing Association and Exhibitor Surveys compiled the following points of interest from surveys of trade show exhibitors and attendees:

1. 80% of fulfillment during and after a show is wasted on unqualified prospects, or thrown away by potentially qualified prospects.
2. The average cost of fulfillment with literature is $10.75.
3. Only 20% of leads ever get followed up at least once!
4. It takes 3.4 phone calls to reach a prospect.
5. It takes 7.6 phone calls to fully qualify or disqualify a prospect.

Therefore, know that there is a cost associated with both GENERATING the lead, and a cost to FOLLOW-UP the lead. Understand that the cost of the show is only a part of your total expense. The wasted literature and lost time spent pursuing your leads also adds to your overall cost.

Your challenge is first to know how much you spend, and then understand "why" you spend this amount. Don't overlook your total costs; factor everything in, using your post-show follow-up costs. Then, share this information with your people to showcase the real values and costs associated with your exhibit marketing.

TRADE SHOWS:
A Profit Center or Money Pit?

The statement, "why bother, why spend the money?" is often said regarding trade shows, especially with the availability of information on the Internet. The prevailing thought in many companies is that trade show marketing is an expensive means to market goods and services, in effect a waste of money. Shows are sometimes called a "vacation" for top management and the sales team. Nothing could be further from the truth. Anyone who has taken part in planning, working, and managing a trade show can tell you that a show is a huge investment in time, energy, and resources.

There is great truth in the wasteful aspects of trade show marketing. The primary reason is the inability to show a tangible return for each show over months and years. With the advent of the Internet, the ability to find vendors, information, and solutions is easier for prospects, providing them with more choices for their needs. More choices mean more competition, more noise, and less distinction in the marketplace. With the availability of information, prospects do not find the same value in attending trade shows, and many choose to get their product information through the use of the Internet.

To make matters worse, corporate downsizing has placed a tremendous burden of additional responsibilities on employees. Companies and employees are now expected to produce more shows and increase show sales with fewer resources. Show budgets have also been reduced or eliminated, while the pressure to justify the trade show investment has increased.

Why Bother?

If you talk to most trade show exhibitors, you will find a common list among those who do not know their returns and results from a show. Most will tell you that they exhibit because:

1. Our competition is there
2. We always go to the show
3. People would talk about us if we did not show
4. We "hope" to get new customers
5. To introduce a new product
6. We don't know why we exhibit

The fact remains that most companies either do not know why they exhibit, or have reasons for exhibiting that do not reflect a plan that works toward any goal or outcome. Without a goal to reach, and a plan to get there, most trade shows become an expensive marketing outflow that continue to frustrate top management.

That is why in most companies, when the talk about spending the money to exhibit at a trade show surfaces, most everyone involved usually takes the approach of "why bother?"

A Very Large Focus Group

To take a more legitimate approach to trade shows and events, you should realize that a show is really nothing more than a really large focus group, under one roof. To take full advantage of the information and opportunities you gather at a trade show, you must conduct strategic planning sessions for a trade show, preferably months or years in advance. Your company should include all inside and outside sales reps, marketing, top management, and any consultants for your trade show booth, plan, and layout.

When conducting strategic planning sessions for a trade show, you should identify your target prospects. Are they small, medium, or large corporations? Do they fit a particular geographic or demographic profile? Do they specialize or generalize in a product or service? Are they the recognized leaders, secondary tier, or up-and-coming players in their industry? You need to have an identified target driving all your planning, qualifying, and presentation of your company at the trade show.

What are your goals for the trade show? Know them in advance. Write them down and distribute them! Think in terms of increasing awareness for your brand or products, identifying competitors, maintaining or increasing sales, making contact with potential partners, morale booster or reward for hard-working and key employees, etc.

What questions do you want to ask, and answers or types of answers do you anticipate from the show?

As a part of your strategy, consider hiring a professional marketing or exhibit firm to "tune-up" the look or layout of the booth, literature or giveaways at the booth. The money spent here should be specific to the type and location of the show attended, with signage and small messages outlining the overt benefits to the customer, consistent with your goals for the show.

Who does your exhibit booth "speak" to? The exhibit must contain a theme with key ideas. Your salespeople and presenters then drive the key ideas home with the layout and presentation. Good themes to consider are "productivity, reliability, best value, different." This shows that you provide goods and services to help the buyer make more money.

When you finally lay out your plan for the show, you want to avoid the "typical approach to shows" as listed below.

The Typical Approach to Shows

1)   Purchase an exhibit space

2)   Ship the booth crates to the exhibit hall

3)   Arrive at the show to set up the booth

4)   Stand in the booth during the show, answering your cell phone
       and talking with your sales reps

5)   Tell attendees about the greatness of your product/service

6)   Hand out pages of expensive product literature

7)   Scan the attendee's badge for their contact information

8)   Pack up the booth at the end of the show

9)   Send the scanned "leads" to the Sales Reps

10)   Hope and pray for sales

Since a big part of a typical show involves giving away literature, know that:

- Literature given at shows rarely, if ever, makes a lasting impact because 82% is thrown away before it gets back to the prospect's office

- A large part of your trade show budget is wasted sending literature to the wrong people or prospects

- Your prospects forget about you after the show because they are not contacted in a meaningful way after the show; the literature is given the responsibility for memory

That is why the age-old practice of indiscriminately giving away product literature at a show wastes your resources; because most attendees do not ever carry it all the way back to their offices or place of business.

In addition, spending time talking instead of listening does not give you the chance to learn about the prospects' true needs, motivations, and more importantly, their behavioral style. Knowing their behavioral style is extremely important for the follow-up process after the show.

If you are going to take the easy way out of dealing with your leads, then it proves to be much easier to just send the leads off to the Sales

Reps and hope that you see something (sales) before the next time the show rolls around.

However, you need to ask yourself: is hoping for sales a better method than planning for sales?

Instead, consider the following points for a successful approach to trade shows as given to us by Dr. Alessandra's colleague from the trade show industry, Gary Beals. According to Gary, a better approach than the typical approach to shows is:

1.   All booth workers need to know their own style

2.   Know your programs and services

3.   Know the needs of event visitors

4.   Relate your specialties specifically to the visitors' needs

5.   Know about similar products and services by other organizations

6.   Demonstrate your products and services in a different and interesting way

7.   Keep booth staff alert and fresh

8.   Keep the display neat and clean

9.   Be confident and enthusiastic

10.   Be courteous to everyone you meet, prospect or not

Even though these points of performance are not directly Platinum Rule related, you can see that having a sharp focus for your booth staff, and showing respect for the needs and presence of the show attendees, gives you the "edge" you need to learn the most information from your large focus group experience.

Do You Sell At Trade Shows?

With the exception of retail-oriented buyer shows for seasonal goods, you don't see many actual sales occurring on the show floor. The sales process for most companies begins months and sometimes years before the actual show, and therefore if a sale is made at a show, it is merely the end result to previous education, trust, and negotiations.

So if most companies do not "sell" at shows, what is the importance of keeping the prospect or customer in your booth for an extended period of time? Is it important to keep them in your booth the maximum time possible in order to keep them out of the booths of your competitors? If so, do you have the right program to keep the customers' interest, and the appropriate personnel to work with them? Without interaction from you, most customers will wander away from your booth without a compelling reason to stay.

To add to the "holding power" of your booth, consider making a special website, or link to your website to upload digital pictures of customers at your booth. Do you have a machine or display that the customer would like to be photographed next to? Do you have any form of interaction that the customer would participate in? If so, get the permission of the customer to take their picture, and then upload it to your site. Give the customer a card, which has the web link, and they will go there to see themselves, and show their co-workers, friends, and colleagues.

Remember when you used to get back a roll of film from developing. What were the first pictures you always found in the pack? The ones of yourself of course, so give your show prospects a chance to see themselves, and brand that experience with you!

Impulse Buying

Although we stated that most companies do not "sell" at shows, if you know the most likely behavioral styles of your prospects and customers, you could still generate great leads and impressive traffic to your booth by appealing to their buying impulses.

An overlooked tip for many exhibiting companies is to offer a small product or service that could "get your foot in the door" with new prospects. Offer something that is subject to "impulse buying," and get the prospect to begin a positive relationship leading to larger and more profitable sales.

Consider the beginning of the relationship between co-authors of this book; Zimmerman and Underation. At the time they met, Zimmerman had a full-service graphics development firm named Zimmer Graphics. Underation had an active sales rep company.

Zimmerman built graphic identities for companies, developed their web sites and on-line businesses, and supplied professional corporate stationary and logos. Underation went to Zimmer Graphics looking for a logo for his company. While the end goal was to sell a corporate image package with a completely new identity, Zimmerman was smart and first sold the easy-entry sale; a business card package.

The success of the business card sale was not in the card; it was in the service and treatment given the customer. Because of offering to sell first a low-dollar investment, and delivering exceptional service over and above what was required for such a small sale, Zimmer Graphics built trust in the small things, and thereby earned the right to engage in discussions for the next level of products and services.

The relationship started by a $150 business card with logo led into thousands of dollars of business, and the eventual writing of this book. Underation eventually bought every other product developed and sold by the Zimmerman, and earned a lifetime friend on a personal, business, and spiritual level.

To bear the success of the "easy entry" approach to selling, you should look at your products/services and pick one out that would appeal to the behavioral style of your target prospect, and then price it at an attractive or ridiculous price point to move. Capture the information on the prospect as a condition for purchase, and use the information on their style and needs to begin a trust and relationship building campaign after the show concludes.

But you will not get that chance unless you can figure out how to make it easy to buy from you, especially at the show. Work on an easy, simple sale, and start the relationship with a "yes" from the prospect.

Remove from Shopping Mode?

Also know that many prospects come to the show to "shop" for information that might lead to solving a problem in their company. Many exhibitors use the time spent with a prospect to get them out of their shopping mode.

We have a recommendation...don't do it!

The reason is that you try too hard and spend more time talking than listening when you try to get someone out of the shopping mode. People sense this pressure from you, and are repelled, rather than attracted.

Remember that you have time on your side with a prospect. Instead, work on identifying their behavioral style, and interact with them in a way that makes them feel comfortable. If you don't try to close the sale, or remove the prospect from the shopping mode, you will be well on your way to a sale that has potential for a lasting relationship. Therefore, use your time to learn about the true needs of the prospect, let them continue their shopping mode, and keep the sales pitches for the day you sell foot massagers and salsa choppers in your booth.

Begin a Relationship

Your time spent interacting with prospects at the show should focus on two basic outcomes:

1. Determine their primary and secondary behavioral styles

2. Gather enough information about their specific problem or situation to move the relationship forward in the weeks and months following the show

When you try to press too hard to "sell" at a show, you miss the opportunity to really get to know the important items for your prospect. Instead of letting the prospect begin to build the trust required for a long-term relationship, you end up with nothing more than sterile contact information.

The foundations for the relationship are vitally important for your Sales Reps. If you take the time to learn whether or not the person is a Director, Socializer, Relater, or Thinker, you give a head start to the sales person when they make their first contacts following the show. Especially powerful impressions are made when you send a "thank you" card to them immediately following the show. You then write the card according to the items of importance for the prospect. (See Platinum Rule cheat sheet under **"Platinum Rules that Pay"** section.)

Prospects are not accustomed to a booth experience that listens rather than sells. If you take the time to build the beginnings of a lasting relationship, you then become the vendor of choice, and move the sales advantage to your Reps.

What Should You Sell at Trade Shows?

A positive, helpful experience with:

1)   Yourself

2)   Your company

That's all you have time for!

Why Your Best Leads Are Thrown Away

When your company spends their valuable resources generating leads from trade shows, advertisements, web pages, etc., the majority of the leads are doomed to end up in the trash can or "dead file" of your sales people. Why does this happen?

When a sales lead is obtained, most companies and their sales people are programmed to harvest the "low-hanging fruit." They hope to find the customer that has an immediate need for their product or service, and tend to focus their sales efforts at converting those "hot" leads into sales without properly qualifying the prospect or building trust.

In reality, many leads come from prospects with longer rather than shorter buying cycles. Most prospects are not ready to buy today. An honest review of your last 100 leads would reveal that most leads from advertisements and trade shows never turn into sales. Instead, the leads are in reality cold and unqualified, and perpetuate a cycle of wasted time and frustration for the company and the salesperson.

If the lead is discarded by your Sales Reps, then what are your chances of getting the future sale? Your chances are not good, unless you get lucky and the prospect remembers something about your company and makes the effort to find you.

In reality, the prospect will eventually buy from the company that maintained contact and built trust with them over the course of their buying cycle.

Also know that salespeople are naturally focused on the sales that will pay their salaries and generate revenue in the shortest amount of time.

But the problem is that most sales or marketing teams do not have a formal system or business process for lead qualification and conversion. Leads are not warmed or qualified before follow-up. Cold leads then become a low-percentage cold call for sales or marketing people. Cold calls are usually a series of discouraging follow-ups. After that, your valuable leads are looked at as "bad leads" and are placed in a dead file or thrown away.

Why this problem? Sales and marketing is not typically structured to move a prospect through the buying cycle. To improve your lead conversions, your company should consider a Business Development team to qualify, profile, and develop a prospect over time. Only when the lead is fully developed and the prospect is high in the buying cycle should you turn the lead over to sales to close the deal.

Can You Show Me the Money?

The payoff is along the road of your selling cycle, at the end of your selling cycle, and for months and years beyond your selling cycle. In other words, systematic, focused approaches to trade show marketing with targeted customers and personalized follow-up will yield consistent and repeatable sales results.

By identifying and targeting your best prospects, then systematically building trust with them, you will see a greater percentage of your leads turn into sales. The "trust-building" approach takes discipline, patience, and a system to execute on behalf of your salespeople. Therefore, companies looking to convert more of their cold, dead leads will make the effort to build the trust with their prospect before ever trying to sell them.

Your best customers were probably developed over time. And what makes them your best customers? Repeat business of course! Can you name your best customers as your friends? For most salespeople, the answer is yes. Therefore, why not use your best customers as advocates to help you cultivate business with your prospects?

- After the prospect moves through your lead conversion system and becomes a customer, leverage the relationship into more business through referrals. Your customers can help you convince more clients to use your products and services, provided you deliver above and beyond your promises.

- Before you can leverage your customer relationships into new business opportunities, you must first remember that each opportunity starts as a qualified prospect. *Realize that the temptation is great to rush the sales process and try to move a prospect as quickly as possible to a sale.* However, this approach is what "turns off" many prospects and does not build a foundation for future business.

At the prospect stage, defenses are still up with each qualified lead. To position you and your company as a "friend," you must give the prospect a human touch in the form of text-only emails, handwritten notes, and the occasional phone call and visit. Only when a prospect realizes you are their helper and not their seller will they lower their defenses and listen to you. At the point the prospect begins to listen to you, they become your "friend."

SECTION II

INSIDERS SECRETS: WINNING WITH ADVANCED PLATINUM RULE STRATEGIES

T his section of the book gives you practical insights to each and every combination of behavior styles you are likely to meet with your customers and prospects. Of greatest importance is the understanding of why certain customers speak, think, and act as they do. When you understand what "makes people tick", it should reduce your stress and uncertainty when you meet and interact with them.

Pay particular attention to the Communication Strategies at the end of this section, outlining the language used and understood by all behavior styles in voicemail, email, letters, and phone conversations. These strategies alone are worth the price of this book, as the art of interpersonal communication in the workplace has been crippled by voicemail barricades and email filters.

You want to know as much about the best ways to quickly gain the trust and confidence of your prospects and customers. Learning these advanced Platinum Rule strategies will put you on the fast-track to more meaningful and consistent dialogues with everyone you meet.

THE AUTOBAHN OR THE SCENIC TOUR:
Direct or Indirect Behaviors

Direct Behaviors

Direct behaviors, you will find yourself on the fast track in a conversation, like driving the Autobahn, or with indirect behaviors you will take the long way around getting to a real issue, like driving the scenic tour. Either way, you just have to be prepared to quickly identify the behavior and then match the pace.

When you are working a booth, it is easy to spot those with the direct behaviors as they usually seek you with an immediate and direct question. Direct people tend to be assertive, fast-paced people who make swift decisions and take risks. They can easily become impatient with others who do not keep up with their pace. As active people who talk a lot, they appear confident and sometimes dominant. Direct people tend to express opinions readily and make emphatic statements.

Direct people are faster paced, more assertive and more competitive than indirect people. More outspoken, talkative, and dominant, direct people are extroverts who focus their attention on interests within their immediate environment.

Direct people may enjoy taking risks and want results now (or yesterday). Risks are a way of life with them. They crave excitement, so they do as much as possible to get it.

Speaking with conviction, fast-talking, direct people like to tell – not ask – about situations. If you want to know the answer, just ask them. They can even become brutally blunt.

Impatient and quick-paced, Direct people jump into things, sometimes netting huge results and sometimes they encounter dramatic disasters. Wherever inclination takes them, their natural tendency is to do their own thing... as long as it includes doing *something*.

Indirect Behaviors

On the opposite side of the Directness spectrum is the quieter and reserved group... the Indirect people. These are the people who come to your booth and ask two or three questions around an issue before they ever ask you about your product or service. However, they are more easygoing, or at least more self-contained in keeping their views to themselves. Indirect people ask questions and listen more than they talk. They typically do not share their opinions or concerns, but are often willing to listen to yours.

Indirect people tend to be more sensitive toward risk: moving cautiously, meditating on their decisions and avoiding big changes. As a result, they often avoid taking bold chances or acting spontaneously. After all, what is the best way to keep from failing? One way is to *do nothing* until you are convinced it will be an improvement. In other words, only do sure things. Sure things result in a higher success ratio, so they are choices that are more attractive for Indirect people.

Indirect people tend to move at a slower, more measured pace than direct people do. For them, "sooner or later" is good enough. They speak and respond more slowly since they are more cautious or stability-focused when considering change. They tend to seek increases in security while looking for ways to reduce fear. If their behavior becomes too measured, detractors (usually Direct people) may view this as dragging their feet, or even lacking interest.

Predictability is more important to such indirect people; so they tend to weigh pros and cons, attend to details and fact-find. Caught in a gray area with no clear-cut guidelines, they usually ask for clarification or permission before they take action. They seek to meet their needs by accommodating the requirements of their environment. They tend to operate according to established formats and rules, so when you make an appointment with an indirect person, you can expect him to show up on time, or possibly be waiting on you!

THE BANQUET OR THE BANK VAULT:
Open or Guarded Behaviors

With Open or Guarded behaviors, you will either learn everything about the other person, like a banquet, or you will have to work hard to get any type of personal information, almost like their thoughts are locked in a bank vault. You can't pry open the bank vault and you shouldn't shut down the open, banquet-style prospect when you meet them. It is amazing what they will serve you if you let them.

The big difference in these two styles is the way they exert control. Direct individuals attempt to control the people around them while indirect types prefer to exercise control in their environment. In addition to Direct/Indirect, the other dimension of observable behavior that people tend to exhibit is Open or Guarded. This second behavioral scale explains the internal motivating goals behind our daily actions. The Open/Guarded dimension relates to *why* we do the things we do in the way we do them.

When combined, these two scales explain both the tendency to reveal our thoughts and feelings, plus the degree to which we tend to support other people's expressions of their thoughts and feelings.

Open Behaviors

Open people are motivated by their relationships and feelings. They are open to getting to know people and they tend to make decisions based on feelings, experiences and relationships.

The Open person is emotionally available and shows it by talking with his body, using more vocal inflections, making continual eye contact, and communicating in terms of feelings more than the Guarded types. Other *Open* clues are animated facial expressions, a large amount of hand and body movement, a flexible time perspective and immediate, non-verbal feedback. Open people also like to tell, or listen to, stories and anecdotes and make personal contact. They are comfortable with emotions and openly express their joy, sadness, confusion and other emotions.

Open types are also more accepting about time usage. Their time perspective is organized around the needs of people first and tasks second, so they are more flexible about how others use their time than the Guarded types. "I'm sorry I'm late," explains an Open person, "but Jimmy was crying this morning because Jason broke his science project. I had to write a note to his teacher and cheer him up before I dropped him off at school."

Guarded Behaviors

Guarded types like to increase their probability of getting the upper hand and decreasing the probability of appearing foolish. Completing tasks and accomplishing their goals motivate guarded types. They usually like to keep their distance, both physically and emotionally.

Guarded people tend to stand further away from you (even when shaking hands) than Open types. They have a strong sense of personal space and they dislike it when someone invades their territory. They feel invaded when you take something from their desk, use personal items without permission, or call meetings (requiring their time) without asking their input.

Guarded people show less facial expression, displaying limited or controlled hand and body movement, and adhere to a more time-disciplined agenda. They push for facts and details, they focus on the issues and tasks; they keep their personal feelings private. They are not naturally "touchy-feely," and they tend to respond stiffly if anyone touches them.

The more Guarded types like structure; they like to know what to expect. Additionally, they prefer to have control over results within a structured environment. When negatively motivated, they can be viewed as coercive, restrictive or overbearing. They prefer to stick with an agenda... at least if it's their own.

DIRECTORS...
The Initiators of Chaos and Action

Of all the styles, the most fast-paced and hard-hitting are the Directors. They initiate change, momentum and growth. The classic definition of a "self-starter" (think Donald Trump). They focus on attaining their goals, and their key need is to achieve their bottom-line results. The driving need for results, combined with their motto of "Lead, follow, or get out of the way," explains their no-nonsense, direct approach to getting things accomplished.

Directors are driven by an inner need to be in personal control. They want to take charge of situations so they can be sure of attaining their goals. They often order for you at a restaurant! Their ultimate goal is the result, the victory, and they're not willing to wait.

The journey is not necessarily the main point of what motivates a Director, especially if it takes too many detours. They want the shortest path to the goal, and will many times run through rather than over the hurdles to get there. Their dream vehicle is an M-1 Abrams tank!

Directors Pursue Achievement and Control

Directors want to win, so they may naturally "challenge" people or practices in the process. They accept challenges, then take over and exert authority while they plunge headfirst into solving the problem. They tend to focus on administrative and operational systems and can work quickly and impressively by themselves. You can really smell the tires burning when a Director starts down the track!

Directors are naturals at being in control. They tend to be independent, strong-willed, precise, goal-oriented, and competitive with others... especially in a business environment. Climbing the corporate ladder is merely a small obstacle course to them! They try to shape their environment en route to their accomplishments. They demand freedom to manage themselves and others, and use their drive to become winners.

Directors like to get things done and make things happen. They start, juggle and maintain many projects concurrently. Their primary skills are their ability to get things done, lead others and make decisions. Directors have the ability to focus on one task... at the exclusion of everything and sometimes everyone else. (The classic definition of tunnel vision.) They can block out doorbells, sirens, or other people while channeling all their energies into the specific job at hand.

Directors are Driven and Expect to Drive

Directors like to move at a fast pace and tend to become impatient with delays. It is not unusual for a Director to call someone and launch into a conversation without saying "Hello." Often, Directors tend to view others who move at a slower speed as less competent, or at least aggravating.

Their weaknesses tend to include impatience, intolerance, poor listening habits and insensitivity to the needs of others. Their complete focus on their own goals and immediate tasks may make them appear aloof and uncaring.

One other thing to remember about Directors is that if you give a concession to a Director, get one in return – concession for concession. You might offer to negotiate new terms and agreements on future sales. *Earning respect with Directors is critical to a long-term relationship!*

Directors are Decisive

Directors embrace challenges, take authority, make decisions quickly, and expect others to do the same. They prefer to work with people who are decisive, efficient, receptive, competent and intelligent.

You may often find Directors in top management positions, and their personal strengths often contribute to their success in jobs such as a hard-driving reporter, a stockbroker, an independent consultant... or a drill sergeant! Under pressure, Directors often get rid of their anger by ranting, raving or challenging others. While relieving their own inner tensions, they often create stress and tension within others.

Director's Style at Work

The Director can be an excellent problem solver and leader. Higher power positions and/or career areas motivate them (situations where they can take charge and get the glory).

Directors realize that results can be gained through teamwork (and may actually develop a management approach that demands and supports teamwork), but it requires adaptation. The nature of the Director is to focus on their individual actions and accomplishments to gain motivation.

Director business characteristics include:

- Controlled timeframes
- Personal control
- Getting to the point quickly
- Persistence and single-mindedness in reaching goals
- Downplayed feelings and relationships

Directors In a Flash

The Director is a person who will act quickly and decisively. They have a need to be recognized for their accomplishments and seek approval for their "victories." The Director will always be concrete in their thinking, choosing the practical approach over the theoretical approach.

Directors want to have facts; lots of facts, and you are best served when the facts are highlighted for them. Directors also embrace change, and in many cases seek change for the excitement of reaching new goals and exploring uncharted ground.

Directors behave in a way that shows low tolerance for the feelings, advice, and attitude of others. A Director is not concerned about bulldozing through other pet projects in quest of the next victory. Rather, they are concerned only about the results, especially for them, not so much the impact of the journey.

SOCIALIZERS...
The Talkers and Hawkers

Socializers are the great talkers because they are friendly, enthusiastic and like to be where the action is. They thrive on admiration, acknowledgement, compliments and applause. They want to have fun and enjoy life. Energetic and fast-paced, Socializers tend to place more priority on relationships than on tasks. They influence others by their optimistic, friendly demeanor and they focus primarily on attaining positive approval from others.

Socializers Need Attention and Approval

Admiration and acceptance are extremely important to Socializers. Often, they are not as concerned about winning or losing as how they look while they're "playing the game." The Socializer's greatest fear is public humiliation: appearing uninvolved, unattractive, unsuccessful or unacceptable to others. These frightening forms of social rejection threaten the Socializer's core need for approval. As a result, when conflict occurs, Socializers may abruptly take flight for more favorable environments.

The Socializers' primary strengths are their enthusiasm, persuasiveness and friendliness. They are "idea-a-minute" people who have the ability to get others caught up in their dreams. With great persuasion, they shape their environments by building personal alliances to accomplish their results. Then they seek nods and comments of approval and recognition for those results. They are stimulating, talkative and communicative.

Socializers are Impulsive

Socializers are generally open with their ideas and feelings, but sometimes only at superficial levels. They are not as prone to "wearing their hearts on their sleeves." They tend to work quickly and enthusiastically with others. They are risk takers and base many of their actions and decisions on natural impulse and feelings. Their greatest irritations are doing repetitive or complex tasks, being alone, or not having access to a telephone!

Their weaknesses are too much involvement in too many projects, impatience, aversion to being alone, and short attention spans. They become bored quickly and easily. They may not thoroughly investigate, assuming someone else will do it, or they may procrastinate because re-doing something just isn't exciting enough. When Socializers feel they do not have enough stimulation and involvement, they get bored and look for something new... repeatedly.

Socializers are Optimistic

Socializers are often found in positions such as sales, public relations specialists, talk show hosts, trial attorneys, social directors on cruise ships, hotel personnel and other people-intensive, high-visibility careers. Audience reactions stimulate them and they thrive in entertainment fields where their natural, animated actions can flow easily. They like to charm friends, co-workers and audiences with their friendliness and enthusiasm.

Socializer's Style at Work

The Big Picture is much more interesting to Socializers than supporting details. After seeing the broad overview, they prefer not to personally dwell on specifics. Their enthusiasm helps them generate many ideas and their tendency to get feedback from everyone around them helps select ideas that have a good chance to succeed.

Socializers are happy working with other people. They like being treated with warmth, friendliness, and approval. Because they favor interacting with people on more than just a business level, they want to be your friend before doing business with you.

The Socializer likes a quick pace and often moves about the office in a flurry of activity. They even walk in a way that reflects their optimism and pace... lively and energetically. They tend to think aloud and often walk around the office talking to almost everyone.

Since Socializers are naturally talkative and people-oriented, dealing with people who are in positions of power meets their need for inclusion by others, popularity, social recognition and relative freedom from a lot of detail.

Socializers' business characteristics include:

- Wants freedom from control, details, or complexity
- Likes to have the chance to influence, persuade or motivate others
- Gets easily bored by routine and repetition
- Typically have short attention spans, so they do better with short communications
- Prefer talking to listening

Socializer's Talking Points:

Above everything, the Socializer craves interaction and human contact. Spontaneous actions and decisions are a part of the Socializer's daily life. More than any of the four styles, the Socializer is concerned with approval and appearances.

The Socializer is an emotion-based decision maker who needs help getting and staying organized. They like the help as it gives them more opportunity for personal interaction.

At the opposite end of the spectrum, the Socializer dislikes conflict and avoids negativity at all costs.

THINKERS...

Analyzers and Roadmap Readers

Thinkers are analytical, persistent and systematic problem solvers. They are more concerned with logic and content than style. Thinkers prefer involvement with products and services under specific, controlled, predictable conditions so they can continue to perfect the performance, process, and results.

If you can recall a Thinker in your life, you might see someone who is often quiet, and not the social hub in your family or friends. But don't confuse someone who is quiet with someone who is not intelligent; rather the Thinkers prove to be very intelligent. But don't ever ask them to explain something to you – unless you have a lot of time to spend hearing the story!

Thinkers Seek Order and Assurances

The primary concern of the Thinker is accuracy; this often means that emotions take a back seat. They believe feelings are more subjective and distort objectivity. Their biggest fear is of uncontrolled emotions and irrational acts, which might prevent the achievement of their objectives. They share a deep fear of being wrong, or at best, incorrect. Thinkers strive to avoid embarrassment by attempting to control both themselves and their emotions. Of the four styles, Thinkers are the most risk-conscious and have a high need for accuracy.

Thinkers make decisions logically and cautiously to increase the probability that they take the best available action. They are deliberate and strive to be technically perfect. Thinkers demand a lot from themselves (and others) and may succumb to overly critical tendencies.

Thinkers tend to keep their criticisms to themselves, hesitating to tell people what they think is deficient or incorrect. They typically share information, both positive and negative, only if requested, or on a need-to-know basis... and only if they have received assurances that there will be no negative consequences to them.

The Thinker tends to be serious, orderly, and is likely a perfectionist. They tend to focus on the more critical details in the process of work and become irritated by surprises or glitches. They like organization and structure, and dislike involvement either with too many people or with any one person for too long a period.

Thinkers Move Slowly

Because Thinkers like to be right, they prefer checking processes themselves. This tendency toward perfectionism, when taken to an extreme, can result in "analysis paralysis." These overly cautious traits may result in worry that the process is not progressing exactly right, which further promotes their tendency to behave in a critical, detached way.

Thinkers may appear to be aloof, meticulous and critical. Their fear of being wrong can make them over-reliant on the collection of information and slow to reach a decision. While Thinkers are natural observers who ask many questions, they may focus too much on downside possibilities and remote dangers... at the expense of missing up-side opportunities and bottom-line payoffs.

In their effort to avoid conflict, Thinkers often refrain from voluntarily expressing their inner thoughts and feelings. This lack of direct feedback may lead to future misunderstandings and weaken relationship-building opportunities.

Thinkers Need Details

Perhaps you live or work with someone who is quiet, individualistic, slow to speak or show emotion, and covets his or her privacy. Oftentimes, there is a lot going on inside their head as they agonize over what to do next, how their feelings operate, and ultimately, the process of doing the right thing. They tend to put their emotions under a microscope then analyze and reanalyze them to make sure their response was proper given the stimulus that set them off.

The Thinker is a contemplator, examining the pros and cons of any given situation and trying to consider everything. Their need to weigh possibilities and ramifications can cause stress for faster-paced behavioral types, and sometimes Thinkers contemplate a situation until the opportunity slips away completely. However, the Thinker's innate caution can serve to offset the more impetuous ideas or decisions made by of some other types.

The Thinker's Style At Work:

In business, Thinkers are the refiners of reality. They seek neither utopias nor quick fixes. Because of their risk-averse tendencies, they may overly plan when change becomes inevitable. Planning is their way of improving their odds. They like working in circumstances that promote quality in products or services. Their thorough preparation minimizes the probability of errors. They prefer finishing tasks on schedule, but not if it might be at the expense of making a mistake. They dislike last minute rushing and inadequate checking or review.

Thinkers prefer logic and rely on reasoning to avoid mistakes. They tend to check, recheck, and check again. They may become mired down with accumulating facts and over-analysis. They are uncomfortable freely giving opinions or partial information until they have exhausted all their resources. This process can frustrate other behavioral types who want to know what is going on *now*.

Business Characteristics of the Thinker:

- Concerned with process; wants to know how something works

- More interested in quality than quantity; prefer lower output to inferior results

- Wants to be right; uses logical thinking processes in order to avoid mistakes

- Dislikes unplanned changes and surprises

Thinker's Points of Logic:

The Thinker is programmed to think logically and analytically. To be logical and analytical, they need data and pose many questions to answer. Thinker will usually ask questions that center around specific details.

The Thinker likes organization and structure. They work slowly and precisely alone, and look to avoid conflict and over-involvement with others. Thinkers are very cautious and do not let many people inside their inner circle of trusted friends.

RELATERS...

The Steady and Dependable Helpers

Relaters are warm, supportive and predictable. They are the most group-oriented of all the four styles. Having friendly, lasting, first name relationships with others is one of their most important desires. They dislike interpersonal conflict so much that when they disagree, they will often keep silent. At other times, they may say what they think other people want to hear. Other people usually feel comfortable interacting with Relaters because of their low-key, non-confrontational nature. Relaters are natural listeners and like to be part of networks of people who share common interests.

Relaters Need Respect and Tranquility

Relaters focus on getting acquainted and building trust. They are inwardly flustered by pushy, aggressive behavior. They are cooperative, steady workers who function well as team members. They strive to maintain stability and to create a peaceful environment for others.

Relaters prefer to stick with what they already know and have experienced. *Risk* is a dangerous word to Relaters. They may even stay in an unpleasant environment rather than take chances by making a change. Disruption in their routine patterns can cause them distress. When faced with a change, they need to think it through slowly, systematically and piece-by-piece in preparing for the change.

The primary strengths of Relaters are their accommodation, appreciation for – and patience with – others. They are courteous, friendly and willing to share responsibilities. They are good implementers who are persistent and will usually follow through on the completion of action plan steps; they do so because they hate to let other people down or fear confrontation.

Relaters Disagree Quietly

Relaters have difficulty speaking up and expressing their true feelings, especially if it might create conflict. They appear to go along with others even when they inwardly do not agree. This tendency creates an environment where the more aggressive types may take advantage of the Relater. Their lack of assertiveness sometimes results in hurt feelings because they do not let others know how they truly feel.

In business and in their personal lives, Relaters take one day at a time and may consciously avoid gambles and uncertainties. Because stability in the workplace motivates them, Relaters have the most compatible of all working relationships with each of the four types. Relaters have patience, staying power and persistence, so they commit themselves to making relationships work.

Relaters are extremely uncomfortable with disagreement, often withholding negative observations. They do not want to make waves and they do not want to appear to be know-it-alls. Silently, they may feel as if they're shouldering the lion's share of the duties, but they are unlikely to complain about this to others.

Relaters are Sensitive

Relaters are quiet, evenly paced and inwardly focused individuals. They recharge their batteries and renew their energy by looking for answers within themselves and a relatively small group of friends, family and associates. As warm and open as they may appear, they have private thoughts that they are reluctant to divulge. Their energy drains when called upon to share how they feel about private matters or controversial topics that may offend someone. They would rather sit back, observe other's feelings, and then offer a more measured response based on their perception about how their opinion would be received. They are naturally tuned in to the overall group dynamics as well as the feelings of the individuals that comprise the group.

Relaters are uncomfortable with intangibles. They dislike deviating from the established, proven order... such as when dealing with abstractions. They prefer instead to follow a predetermined, straightforward procedure. They are on firm ground when working with concrete realities such as known products, people, systems and procedures.

Business Characteristics of the Relater:

- Needs to know the order of procedures; fears the unknown
- Slow and steady; builds strong and deep relationships, but with fewer people
- Motivated by customary, known, proven practices
- Focuses on how and when to do things
- Likes a long-term relationship with fellow employees

Relater's Relative Points:

- Concerned with stability
- Needs personal involvement
- Takes action and make decisions slowly
- Needs to know the step-by-step sequence
- Avoids risks and changes
- Dislikes interpersonal conflict
- Wants to know they are appreciated

A PRODUCT OF YOUR ENVIRONMENT:
Strong Clues to Behaviors

Look at your customer's office. How is it decorated and arranged? What items are on the desk? Is it messy, organized into neat piles or spotlessly clean? What types of things are on the walls and in their bookshelf? What seating arrangement does this customer seem to prefer and find most comfortable?

Environmental clues offer important information, but should not be used as the sole basis for determining one's style. In many situations, environment may be determined more by the culture of the organization than by your client. Looking for environmental clues is a way to enhance and corroborate the identification made by observing behavior. This observation also helps you glean clues about an organization's culture and style.

Director Environments

A Director's desk is likely to be busy with paperwork, projects and material separated into organized piles. Both their in-baskets and out-baskets typically bulge with busywork. They also tend to surround themselves with trophies, awards, photos, and other evidence of personal achievement. Everything about this office signals hustle, bustle, formality and power.

The Director's preferred power decoration generally includes a large chair behind a massive desk, providing separation from visitors. Walls often display plaques, degrees, awards and other evidence of success as well as large event calendars or project tracking charts.

Directors are more formal and prefer to keep their distance physically and psychologically. They are sensitive about their personal space and do not like to have people get too close. The typical office arrangement is formal with seating that is face-to-face with a big "power desk" separating the Director from his visitors.

Socializer Environments

Socializers respond to visual stimuli, so they like to have everything where they can see it. Consequently, their desks often look cluttered and disorganized and they may even pile paperwork and files across their desk and even onto the floor.

Their walls usually display awards and displays of their current interests. These might include motivational or upbeat slogans or posters, cartoons, drawings or quotations. You may see reminder notes posted and taped all over the place with little apparent forethought, rhyme or reason. Socializers, if asked, will take great pride to explain to you all the things that are on their desk or on the wall because it gives them a chance to talk about themselves and their interests.

Typically, the preferred decor of the Socializer office would be an open, airy, lively atmosphere that represents the personality of its occupant. Likewise, the furniture arrangement indicates warmth, openness and contact. The Socializer does not like barriers such as a desk to separate him from others when he talks. He prefers comfortable, accessible seating, enabling him to meet his goal of getting to know people better.

Thinker Environments

When you walk into an office that is free from clutter, neatly organized, and notice that the desk is clear except for one file, a phone and maybe a computer, you are likely to be in Thinker territory. Thinkers like neat, highly organized desks unimpeded by clutter. Everything in the Thinker's office has its rightful place... almost to the point of being preordained.

The office walls of Thinkers contain their favorite types of artwork: charts, graphs, exhibits, models, credentials or more formal, job-related pictures.

Thinkers favor a functional decor that enables them to work more efficiently. They tend to keep most resources within reach... readily available whenever needed.

Thinkers are non-contact people who prefer the formality of distance. This preference is reflected in the functional arrangement of their desks and chairs, usually with the desks physically separating you from them. Although they may not keep eye contact with you, do not interpret this to mean they are not interested in what you may be selling. Unemotional, disengaged behavior is common for those who are "Indirect" and "Guarded."

Relater Environments

Relaters' desks contain pictures of family and friends along with other personal items. Their office walls display conservatively framed personal slogans, family or group photos, serene pictures or mementos. They surround themselves with nostalgic memories of stabilizing experiences and relationships. These remembrances of a pleasant, uncomplicated past allow them to transform their offices into a warm, friendly cocoon that shields them from a fast-paced, ever-changing world.

They prefer to arrange seating in a side-by-side, more congenial, cooperative manner... no big "power desks" for them! If they do have a big desk though, they will usually walk out from behind it to greet their visitors. Colors and furniture selections are generally conventional and conservative in tone.

In addition to family photos and pictures, you may find certificates recognizing the Relater for their volunteer hours for various hands-on activities in the community or business. Relaters typically enjoy giving their time for causes they feel strongly about. This satisfies their need to give, and provides them an opportunity to meet more potential friends and to see what is going on behind the scenes.

SPEAK THEIR LANGUAGE:
Voicemail, Email, Letters

Sometimes you do not get a chance to see your client in person and contact may be limited to an email, phone conversation or a letter. Even these limited communications can offer you clues to the customer's style. The following information will help you determine their behavior style early in the relationship and allow you to treat the "patient" the way they want to be treated.

Director's Emails, Letters and Memos

Director's correspondence tends to be brief and to the point. They may mention highlights of conversations or materials, but they do not detail them unless necessary. They generally include specifics for your follow-through or raise questions they want answers to... *now!* Even notes and cards take on abbreviated forms and with little or no strong feelings and/or tone expressed.

Socializer's Emails, Letters and Memos

Look for exclamation points, underlining and bold highlighting. If it's an email, you might find unusual fonts, several colors and graphics. In their text, you can almost hear the Socializer emphasizing those emotion-laden, picturesque adjectives and adverbs. Socializers write in the same stimulating, energetic way that they speak. Socializers' letters often include personal anecdotes or references to shared experiences. Socializers are famous for their postscripts and might even include a "P.P.S.: ____"

Thinker's Emails, Letters and Memos

Thinkers send letters that seek to clarify positions and address processes. Consequently, they may become rather long and filled with information and questions, while at the same time being somewhat indirect and intentionally obtuse. A second type of Thinker letter is a short communiqué with an accompanying host of enclosures, citations or references. The purpose of their letters is to process information in ways that maintain or enhance their position.

Relater's Emails, Letters and Memos

Relaters send letters to update people or keep in touch and let you know they're thinking of you. Relaters like to send thank you notes for almost anything: inviting them to an office party, bringing lunch back for them or including them on a company function. They may even send a thank you note to acknowledge your thank you note. You can count on holiday season cards from them every year as long as you remain on their "relationship" list.

On the Phone with a Director

Again, the Director prefers to be brief and get right to the point... especially when it's their time or your agenda! They may start the conversation with whatever they are focused on... with no personal acknowledgement or greeting. They often speak in a sort of shorthand – concisely or at least pointedly – and sound cool, confident and demanding. They tend to speak loudly, rapidly and emphatically... and view phones as task command devices. You may get the sense that they are not hearing what you are saying. Be sure to measure what you say, as they may later replay the conversation later in their head. If something seemed amiss about what you said it could shake their confidence in you and cost you a sale.

On the Phone with a Socializer

"What's up?" "What's happening?" or "How's it going?" are common Socializer opening lines. Their animation and gestures come straight through the phone line as if they're in the room with you. Socializers love the phone and recharge their batteries by talking to others. They speak rapidly with a lot of emphasis and emotion; they can talk longer and better than the other styles. When calling you from a shaky cell phone connection, they may talk for two or three minutes before they even realize the call was dropped. For them, phones are instant "airlines" for transporting them anywhere and anytime for a visit with others.

On the Phone with a Thinker

The Thinker is formal, time-conscious and uses the phone as a tool to process tasks whenever necessary. They prefer brief to-the-point telephone calls. Thinkers tend to express themselves in a rather tentative manner and display caution in making commitments in phone conversations. Thinkers speak in a careful, soft manner with non-emotional delivery. While the phone does give them the option to avoid face-to-face involvement, they may perceive unscheduled phone calls as an invasion of their privacy, time and/or a disruption from their work.

On the Phone with a Relater

Relaters greet people warmly on the phone, asking, "How are you?" and expressing pleasure at hearing from you. They immediately put you on a first-name basis and patiently listen to your ideas and feelings. Relaters talk more slowly and quietly with a steady, even-tempered delivery. They enjoy listening, since it affords them another avenue to best understand and respond to others; the phone is a valued tool for Relaters.

Wrapping up...

Environmental clues will help you confirm your style identification of the people around you: clients, co-workers, friends and family. Once you are comfortable that you understand their style, you can begin to communicate with them on their own wavelength... in their own style. The next section explains two fundamental adjustments you can make to improve your communication with anyone you meet. It also provides you with strategies for improving your effectiveness with your customers at each step of the sales process.

SECTION III

THE TRADE SHOW MASTERY SYSTEM USING PLATINUM RULES

In this section, we give you the complete view of professional, systematic trade show event sales and marketing using The Platinum Rule.

Too often, trade show and event budgets do not take into account the pre-show and post-show components of the mix. When you only spend your time, money, and efforts into producing and executing on the show or event floor, you miss the pre and post-event functional areas and your overall results will suffer.

You will build a complete program and increase your results when you use The Platinum Rule in your pre and post-show prospect and customer dealings. In addition, you will certainly gain a dramatic increase in the ease which you meet your ultimate show goals.

The added benefit to viewing shows and events as a "three-act play", each with distinct and important parts, will steamroll your exhibit and event program results over any and all of your competitors.

BRIGHT LIGHTS, BIG CITY:
Thriving Trade Shows are a Three-Act Play

During the preparation of a typical trade show, most of the energy and budget is directed onto the show floor, not taking into account any target marketing before the show or systematic lead follow-up after the show. Neglecting the pre- and post-show sales and marketing short circuits the potential to maximize your return on show investment through the identification, cultivation, and conversion of your leads into customers.

It is important to understand that a trade show is like a three-act play, and is broken into three distinct parts:

Act One: Pre-show marketing and planning

Act Two: At-show execution of your strategies and tactics

Act Three: Post-show lead follow-up and relationship building

These three distinct parts represent an act of the trade show "play." Any play without the beginning, middle, and final acts will probably not last long on the stage, let alone Broadway. There is neither anticipation nor follow-through to the production. Any attempt to "do" a show, focusing only on Act Two, the at-show execution, will usually net a frustrating set of results.

It is when a company allocates their marketing budgets for the pre- and post-show parts that they move to realizing their full potential from trade shows. The following sections will outline the considerations of each act of the trade show "play."

ACT ONE, PRE-SHOW:
Draw Bull's-eyes, Don't Herd Cats

For pre-show marketing and planning, you must understand that your best opportunities to attract quality prospects resides in your ability to attract them prior to the show and to get their commitment to visit you during the show.

There are many programs available to attract your best prospects prior to the show, such as coordinated email, mail, and phone call campaigns, but the question arises of *whom* you will target.

Targeting your prospects prior to the show is the key to success. Start with asking your sales people for their list of key accounts or key prospects. Each and every salesperson should be able to provide you with a list of prospects and customers they need to see at the show. Get this list at least three months prior to the show and plan on "touching" each person at least five or six times leading up to the show.

- Your goal is to get them to respond to your marketing and schedule an appointment to meet with your key people on the show floor.

- Offer an incentive to attend, in the form of a free giveaway that can be redeemed only at your booth.

- If you are targeting high-level executives, you will expect to spend $50 or more on the gift.

- Make sure the gift is of value to the attendee, maybe in the form of an MP3 player, or a USB storage card that has your products and services imbedded in a file form.

- Have your staff call two weeks prior to the show to confirm their attendance, and get the meeting scheduled.

You want the pre-show activities to really have targets with names and faces associated with them. At the very least, you want a likely behavioral style or styles that you will develop your marketing messages around. Draw the bull's-eyes on specific people; put them on your "platinum" list of high-value prospects.

It is the company that does not take this defined focus, instead casting a wide net in hopes of snaring someone, anyone that finds itself in the difficult position of herding cats. As we all know, cats have a mind of their own, and so do show attendees. So if you choose to herd cats, at least make sure they are all of a similar breed!

ACT TWO, AT-SHOW:
Be the Pincushion, Not the Needle in the Haystack

You want to be both the person and the company who prospects and customers place on their "must-see" list when they plan their route on the show floor. You want to be the pincushion that everyone will "stick" as they walk the aisles. Being the pincushion is a result of a well-executed, targeted, pre-show marketing campaign.

Don't go to the show knowing you are the "needle in the haystack." That is when you hope that you will stumble upon a prospect that might be a good fit for you, and that you will find them in the sea of attendees as though they were the proverbial needles in a haystack. Not good odds on your part.

For attendees who make you their pincushion, use the face time at the booth not to sell, but to gather and *record* any information you may need to further the sales process following the show. You may want to find out their specific wants or needs for your products and services, any budgets that may be available, time frames for purchase, and all the decision makers involved.

Ask about the prospect's situation in the brief time you have with them. Educate when asked, and save your sales pitch for later in the follow-up process.

- Have the discipline to attract the right prospects. Don't confuse a crowded booth with a lower-volume booth of quality prospects.

- Do not confuse high lead quantity numbers with a good show.

The key to working the show is to build the information you need to move the sales process forward immediately following the show. Therefore, you must *record* your information gathered into a system to use for post-show marketing and relationship building. "Branding" at the show is fleeting and confusing, so consider the show floor as your giant focus group for gathering information.

ACT THREE, POST-SHOW:
Where Are the Leads?

As indicated in a previous section, the typical reaction to post-show leads is to merely sort them and deliver them to your Sales Reps by territory. After that, you hope for some sort of follow-up or lead development on their part, something that might lead to an eventual sale. But the reality is that most of these leads are lost in the daily activities of the salesperson, and the prospect will come back at the next show, wondering why you and your company did not care enough to help them.

Instead of handing out the leads to the Sales Reps, consider keeping them in-house and developing them for your salespeople, from the corporate or Business Development side. Why? Because post-show lead follow-up and relationship building is your best opportunity to "brand" your products and services on behalf of your salesperson.

If you know and understand that 80% of your attendees will probably not have an immediate need, you will have the opportunity to build your brand over weeks, months, and even years after the show. You support your sales team by providing the prospect with helpful information about their needs, and not trying to blatantly sell to them. The goal is to build the relationship and position your company as their first choice when ready to buy. That is the goal of true branding.

The key to accomplishing post-show "branding" is to use a system that will automatically deliver most of the marketing for your salesperson. Consider this process as Business Development, and treat the development of the prospect's trust as your first goal. When you show your consistent determination to stay in touch with the prospect, and your willingness to help them and not SELL them, they will view you as the people they're most likely to give the first opportunity to work a deal when the time arises.

Smart exhibitors will find a system that takes a behavioral style based approach to their pre- and post-show marketing, while also requesting permission of their prospects to help them after the show is over.

Why get that permission or commitment? It is too easy for a prospect to delete unsolicited emails, discard generic flyers and catalogs, and hide behind voicemail. Short of taking expensive trips to see each and every prospect, the first step beyond initial prospect qualification is to ASK the prospect for permission to stay in touch, and learn the method and timing that suits them. Have them agree to let you in, and they most likely will. Too many people are out to steal a person's time these days, and time is extremely limited in today's workplace.

The reality is that a first-rate lead conversion system takes time to properly develop and implement. There is work involved! In many cases, the effort is a total overhaul of the traditional methods a company is comfortable using. However, the rewards are great for those companies and individuals who take the time to identify their ideal prospects, then use a laser focus, over time, to build the trust and relationships that lead to long-term relationships and continual sales.

THE BIG AUDITION:
Leverage Pre-Show Success with Platinum Planning

You never really know what may or may not happen on the show floor, but you must always be prepared to make the best of it, rather than complain and blame your problems on someone else.

In this section, we discuss the things that you should "iron out" when you prepare for a show. Pre-show marketing, calls, mailers, staff training, and dress rehearsals all play a part in improving the likelihood of your success at a show. Also, a part of many show exhibits is a presentation or training in the booth. As any seasoned booth presenter knows, things can and usually do take an unexpected turn, and when you do any training at your booth during the course of a show, the unexpected can be expected to happen.

An example of unexpected turns came for Dr. Sheila Murray Bethel. As a consultant, she was asked to make a sales presentation to her client's group at a construction industry trade show. She willingly accepted, went to the show hall and looked for the room she was assigned for her part of the program.

To her surprise, she found that her sales presentation was to take part in the client's booth, on the show floor! Since she did not know her part was taking place on the show floor, there was no opportunity for Platinum Planning. Instead, it was a recipe for disaster.

To complicate matters, Sheila found that her client's booth was between an exhibitor giving away ice cream cones and another exhibitor demonstrating their latest and greatest nail gun! Every time the gun went off, everyone jumped an inch and immediately turned their attention to the other booth.

The final insult was the ice cream giveaway. Attendees not with her client's group kept wandering into the booth, eating their ice cream, wanting to hear the "presentation." One man even brought his newspaper and sat in the front row, eating his ice cream while reading the paper!

Sheila described the presentation as the longest hour of her career. Even though she got high marks from the client, and even a "good ideas" comment from the newspaper reader in the front row, the scene was still one of mass confusion.

When introducing yourself to a Director, sound confident and increase your pace while you speak: *Mr. Smith, this is Joe Jones with Acme Computer. I just spoke to a business associate of yours, Ted Stevens. He told me you might be in the market for our training services because they will give your business an edge over the competition and increase your bottom line. When would be a good time to meet with you to discuss how I might help your business secure a distinct advantage over your competitors?*

When introducing yourself to a Socializer, lean forward, smile into the phone, and ramp up your pace: *Hi, Mr. Smith, this is Joe Jones with Acme Computer. I just spoke with Ted Stevens, who told me that you might be interested in our training packages because they are fun, innovative and effective. I'd like to swing by next week to meet you. I really think we'll be able to help you and your business. Perhaps we could meet over lunch? What's your availability?*

When introducing yourself to a Relater, lean back in your chair, relax, smile and slow down your pace: *Hi, Mr. Smith. This is Joe Jones with Acme Computer. I just spoke with Ted Stevens, and he told me that you'd likely be willing to help me out. I was wondering if we could meet so that I could share some of the ways our training service has helped people just like you develop and enjoy stronger relationships with their customers. Would you be kind enough to meet with me in the next day or two?*

When introducing yourself to a Thinker, sit straight in your chair, slow your pace, and speak clearly: *Good morning (afternoon), Mr. Smith. My name is Joe Jones, and I'm with Acme Computer. I just spoke with Ted Stevens, who told me you might be interested in our training services because they will help your office run more efficiently. I would like to meet with you and take 15 minutes of your time to describe six of the specific ways we could help your business. When would be a convenient time for us to meet?*

If you have to leave voicemail, listen to their outgoing message and do exactly what they ask, regardless of the style. If they say, "...leave your name, number, and brief message," then do exactly that. If they say, "...leave your name, number, and a message of any length," then feel free to do that, too. The rule of thumb is not to leave a message that gives away so much information that they will be able to make a decision on your invitation before ever speaking with you in person.

When in doubt, hang up, think about what you just heard on the message, determine the likely style, and then call back and leave the right type of message.

After listening to the instructions about the type of message to leave on the answering machine, you might consider leaving the *type* of message that speaks to their style. **Note:** the tone and pace should be the same as when speaking to them in person, as noted earlier in this section.

In the above examples, notice the benefit statement given. The purpose of the initial benefit statement is to show a prospect (quickly) what the benefits would be to them. This will give them a reason to talk to you. It makes sense to tell your prospects up front rather than wait until you're halfway through the sales process. Most customers, *regardless of their behavioral style*, are benefit oriented. They may be concerned with cost and interested in features, but their need is always based on the benefits they can gain.

The purpose of making contact with your prospect is to open up lines of communication and plant the benefit seeds prior to the show. The relationship (and the sale) requires the establishment of credibility and the building of trust. When prospects know you sincerely have their best interests in mind, the rest of the process can continue. Today's buyers are appreciative of professionals who show an interest in them, their businesses, their goals and their lives.

Regardless of the style of any prospect, every person you encounter will respond positively to an attentive, patient and intelligent listener. The best way to build rapport with anyone is to ask interesting questions and aggressively listen to their responses. Unfortunately, we strive to improve how we present our ideas, but rarely do we learn how to listen and connect with others.

Start With Better Leads

With the hectic pace on a show floor, it is almost impossible to completely qualify each prospect lead. To improve the initial quality of your leads, train your booth personnel in good questioning and listening techniques. You want to quickly separate prospects from suspects. Resist the temptation to pitch your products and services and indiscriminately swipe show badges.

Have a short list of questions ready to determine the prospects' reason for attending the show, what they are looking for, what they do, what their company does, and the challenges they face. Try to learn as much as you can about the prospects' situation in the brief time you have with them. Educate when asked, and save your sales pitch for later in the follow-up process.

Have the discipline to attract the right prospects. Don't confuse a crowded booth with great prospects.

Do not confuse lead quantity with a good show. Clearly state your purposes to booth staff in gathering show leads. Long term and short term buying cycle leads. Your purpose will tie into your ability to measure results.

The Privilege of Working the Booth

This is an area that is completely misunderstood by exhibiting companies. The basic practice of staffing your booth with sales people, a representative or two from management, and a tech-savvy person to handle the "hard" questions no longer resonates on the show floor. The reason it does not resonate is because the typical booth staff views the experience in the booth as a "duty" and not the privilege it really is.

We outlined earlier the need to foster relationships, build trust, and gather important information about the prospect and their true needs while at the show. Therefore, the adage of staffing your booth with salespeople, intent on "closing" orders or finding prospects high in the buying cycle does not fit the new purpose of your booth time. And as a general rule, salespeople view time in the booth as a duty, and not a privilege.

Consider selecting some of your inside people, folks in customer service, shipping, even production operators in Platinum Rule training, and let them staff your booth and interact with your prospects. These folks are not bent on selling, and with Platinum Rule training will instead focus on identifying styles, gathering information, and building relationships to move the sales process forward. These folks will see that working the booth is a privilege, and accomplish the goal you set before them.

Of course you will get resistance from your salespeople, and downright mutiny from many. But if you select and schedule your salespeople for particular shows, and stress the privilege of working toward the common goals at the show, you will find that past practices will change, and in-booth "selling" will be replaced with listening.

If your salespeople still balk at this practice, or do not comply with the program to identify, listen, and learn, then just remove them from consideration in future shows.

Salespeople are the types that want to be included in events by their very nature. If you set the expectations, and limit the participation to the few you want, you will get the results you desire.

Just have the backbone to carry out the plan, despite the complaints from those who don't like change, and your results will improve.

Pre-show Training and Strategy

To have highly effective booth staff with your targeted prospects and customers, you should identify them *in advance*, and make them familiar to those staffers working your booth. Have your staffers be aware of their companies and names, and the reason you want to speak with them at your booth. Teach your people to NOT sell the prospect once you meet them at the booth, but instead learn as much as they can about that person and their true needs, timetables, budgets, etc. But again, don't go for the sale unless you have already had a project working with that person, and they initiate the sales discussions.

Remember also to identify to your booth workers, *in advance*, any key competitors you may have. Spend extra time with the non-sales staffers who may not know these folks. Be aware that your competitors will want to see your products, services, and messages even more than your prospects, and you need a predefined way to deal with these people, and show your professionalism while doing so.

The best way to show professionalism with your competitors, and still keep them at bay, is to train your people to be polite to your competitors, even praise them for their products. During the praise, be also aware to not offer much in the way of information or giveaways. Keep your conversations with a competitor brief and light. Avoid any confrontations in or around your booth with a competitor, even if they try to provoke you. Remember, the prospects near your booth identify their experience with you, not the competitor. Do not give the competitor a reason to try to injure you or your company. Be the consummate professional, always.

The Platinum List of Prospects and Customers

Every company should have a "Platinum List" of prospects and customers. These are the 20% of people that represent 80% of your current and/or potential business.

Each salesperson and top-level manager should be able to help compile this list. Why bother? Because each person on the list should be profiled to their behavioral style, compiled with as much personal information and interests as possible, and a Platinum Rule-based follow-up program should be put in place to warm, inform, and help make and keep these people happy beyond expectations with your people and your company.

If you do not have a Platinum List to target, you won't be able to identify the highest source of your current and potential income. But when you do, all that you understand of each style will get an opportunity to be put into practice over the months and years you cultivate and enjoy the relationship.

When you have at least 80% of your best 20% clients on-board as loyal and repeat customers, you can then review your lowest paying, highest problem customers and determine if it makes sense to continue your business relationship. Don't be afraid to "fire" a customer. Make sure you have the determination to give your best time and energy to those customers who not only appreciate you for your products and services, but pay you well as a result. Those customers that don't should not be on your Platinum list, or any other current list of your customers. Help them to "move on," rather than annoy your people and waste your resources.

Energizing your Staffers

Your people will be part of a coordinated effort to engage, listen, learn, and report the information they hear from your prospects and customers. Their efforts indeed take a lot of planning, and part of the planning process has to do with their physical and mental health.

When discussing the "energizing of staffers," most people think of pep talks. The reality is that pep talks or motivational talks are merely 1/3 of the process of energizing your staffers. Here is how the major parts of the process break down:

1. Motivational talks by top management to reinforce goals and purpose

2. Proper scheduling of booth time to allow for adequate breaks and rest

3. Rewards, payments and praise for show goals met and exceeded

Most great staffers find their energy in actions, not words. We can tell you that if your Stage Manager or Booth Captain is a Director or Socializer, they should take their high-energy, socially engaging selves into the booth to serve as examples of energy in action. Words alone in the form of pep talks will not do it.

Also noted is the scheduling of time for your people. Try not to wear them out by making them work straight eight-hour days on their feet. Instead, plan adequate rest periods where the staff can take time out to eat a sit-down meal, rest, drink some water, and return their calls and emails. You will enjoy greater performance when your staffers come back rested and relaxed.

Finally, make a public display of gifts, bonuses, or even cash payouts when your show goals, whatever the goals, are met or exceeded. Harvey Mackay said in his book _Swim with the Sharks without Being Eaten Alive_ that cash motivates, especially cash given publicly. Make a show among your peers; honor your people for a job well done. They will find energy from your praise, and their own sense of pride in a job well done.

Dress Rehearsals and Hecklers

You know that practice makes perfect, and the preparation of your staffers with a dress rehearsal is the "missing link" that should be a part of your show team prep.

Most attendees who find their way to your booth either intentionally or by chance will exhibit similar mannerisms. They want to learn more about how you can help make their lives better, and solve some of their problems. If you identify in advance the most likely two behavioral styles of prospect and customer, you can have your people work with questions and scenarios that will convey your message. Certainly you will have every staffer able to answer the "so, what does your company do?" question. And you want to be able to answer with a benefits oriented response with specifics.

For example, if you are a roofing supplier, you would want your people to tell the attendee that you are 12% faster in installation, guarantee to protect your buildings for at least 20 years, and do it at a savings of 32% per roll over the lifetime of the roof. That would certainly get greater attention than telling folks you "make and sell roofing material." Get specific! People want to hear the "what's in it for me" stuff.

Now, also plan for the "bad questions" you may get, especially if your company was or is involved in some sort of a scandal or bad press situation. You want to make sure to give "hecklers" the information YOU want the outside world to have, and therefore control your flow of media.

Without practice, even the most seasoned Platinum Rule veteran could freeze like a deer in the headlights from these types of questions. Practice in situations under pressure for both the good and the bad questions, and have your people ready!

THE CURTAIN RISES:
Use Platinum Guidelines to Reduce Show Stress

When the show finally opens and your big day has arrived, the stress of meeting your high expectations is sometimes tough to handle. That is where the help, reassurance, and direction of Platinum Guidelines can give you a leg-up on your competitors, ease your stress, and lead you to better overall show results. In this section, we review the important guidelines to use at the show, and give you the tools and direction to remain as stress-free as possible.

Among the items that may cause you stress at the show include a damaged or incomplete booth, new offerings from your competitors, broken or damaged products, missing materials, lack of foot traffic, etc. However, you will avoid much of your stress when you come to the show prepared, with goals, a game plan and purpose, have trained employees, use proper forms, and implement your strategies and tactics to achieve them. Although it's not easy to completely eliminate show stress, when you follow the guidelines listed in the following sections, you can drastically reduce the impact of stress and stay focused on your success plan.

Another way to reduce show stress and stay on-target to your goals is to use a seasoned Trade Show Consultant. A proven Trade Show Consultant to work directly in your booth is worth consistently investing a percentage of your show budget.

Having a consultant observing the activities of the people in your booth offers you a view from the visitors' perspective. You will gain insight into the ways your people can improve on an immediate basis, and thus you'll have an opportunity to meet and exceed your pre-show goals.

One expert in analyzing at-show opportunities is Doug MacLean. Doug is President of MacLean Marketing, a trade show consulting firm located in South Carolina. Doug's expertise is working with clients to maximize the performance of their people through improved words, dialogue, and action at trade shows and events. We owe many of the ideas and techniques in this section of the book to his advice and expertise.

As a nationally recognized trainer, speaker, and author, Doug has served hundreds of clients at more than 550 trade shows in the U.S. and around the world. While he has many stories of client work that illustrate his techniques, he tells stories about the value of observation and change at trade shows, resulting in immediate and significant improvement. From merely changing the position of key products in the exhibit to altering the delivery of product messages, his techniques create positive, immediate change for the exhibitor.

Your Booth is your Stage

At a trade show, you are on display. You must make the choice of being an active exhibitor, or a passive exhibitor. Either you let the show come to you, or you take your company's people and message to the visitors. It is the companies that take the proactive rather than reactive approach to trade show prospects that gain the benefit of controlling what happens on their stage, as well as the actors and audience taking part in their play.

Since most of your visitors come to the show on the first day, you gain control of your destiny at the show by your pre-show preparation. Exhibitor studies show that 50%-55% of total show attendees come the opening day. You can't afford to learn your stage and your role on the first day because you lose valuable time and opportunities. After all, there is no spring training for trade shows!

That is why rehearsals are so important. You can't just show up at the opening night of a Broadway show and expect to have a smoothly operating cast, just as you can't expect to have a smooth opening day result in your booth without practicing your interaction with likely behavior styles of your prospects or attendees.

It is advisable to practice these rehearsals under the pressure of a "game day" environment. To do so, you need to put together a detailed set of rehearsal instructions for everyone involved. The key here is not to embarrass any of the players in front of their peers. Remember, you are there to help your teammates, not treat them as the enemy.

You may practice your interactions with products, people, using an interactive kiosk at your booth. If you are able, bring in furniture, flipcharts, video, audio, lighting, or whatever you can do to simulate the influences your people experience in the show setting. It is ideal to practice your interactions with your booth team, within the booth set-up offsite.

If your people give presentations, make absolutely sure they are professionally trained in delivering them, and have the time and opportunity to practice the presentation well in advance of the show. Have the presentation become second nature to your people, and give them praise and feedback to improve their effectiveness.

Make sure your exhibit and people are approachable. Make it easy for prospects or customers to enter your booth, and have your people helpful, but not too aggressive. Do not set physical or perceived barriers at the entrance, unless you intentionally want to screen those who would enter your space. Avoid gimmicks or loud, annoying stunts that will capture the passing attention of an attendee, startle them, and cause them to avoid your booth. Low-pressure sales approaches, combined with a use of the prospect's name (assuming it is listed on a show badge), will pay dividends.

If you know the most likely styles of your prospects, then make your signage reflect a Platinum style message that resonates with your audience. Don't clutter the signage with slogans or claims to attract all four behavioral styles. Instead, pick the top two most likely styles. Whether it is Directors and Thinkers, or Relaters and Socializers, or any combination, just make your booth messages speak to your targeted behavioral styles.

Key words, phrases, or themes to attract the different styles are:

Directors: Efficiency, Cost Savings, Time Savings, Increased
Speed, Analysis

Thinkers: Logical, Process, System, Quality, Guarantee,
Descriptions, Accuracy

Socializers: Quick, Fun, Enjoyable, Testimonials, Spontaneous, Less
Structure or Formality

Relaters: Harmony, Group Involvement, Friendly, Casual,
Trusting, Pleasant

Also make sure your people practice the fine art of quickly identifying other behavioral styles, and the means to adapt to that style. Easiest is when you have a team member represent a style, and let your people practice identifying the style and quickly adapt. The time you spend training to identify and adapt to your prospects and customers will pay great dividends in your show results, and help in the overall process of reducing show stress.

The Role of the Stage Manager

Your Stage Manager is the person in charge of your overall operations in your booth. Moving the team members in and out, providing the flow of information for the prospects and customers, getting any missing or required items to the booth on time; i.e. the overall master decision maker. Some companies call this person a booth captain, but we like Stage Manager since your booth is really a stage used for your show performance.

Remember, your stage is designed to engage and hold the audience while your staff qualify and disqualify with pre-planned questions. Engagement is the primary purpose of the stage, but not the primary purpose of the Stage Manager. Instead of engaging the audience, the Stage Manager should stand back and take an observer's role, not a participant's role. Let him or her interact with the audience, but do not let him or her be the primary contact at your booth. Allow the Stage Manager the freedom to observe the reactions of your prospects, your people, take notes, and prepare any mid-course corrections to your tactics.

As you probably thought, Directors are the best at the role of Stage Manager. They make decisions quickly with the goal or result in mind. Thinkers may be too slow for this job. Relaters might consider the "feelings" of others and not be tough when needed. Socializers could be the second-best style for this job.

The Stage Manager will assemble staff working the booth. The Stage Manager will also conduct your practice meetings and rehearsals, all of which could and should be done well before the show to allow for practice and reflection. At the very least, practice the day before the show opens. It is too late to conduct practice meetings and rehearsals the morning of the show, in a hotel conference room, or especially at your booth in earshot of your competitors.

You may also have very targeted meetings for daily strategies, specific points or key people. These meetings can be held on the morning of the show, but again, it is best to conduct these at least a day in advance if possible. If you are doing the meetings the morning of the show in a public place, be sure to know the people around you at all times. You never know when your competitor or their customers may be near. Therefore, be cautious where you plan the location.

The Stage Manager or Trade Show Consultant should lead the daily strategy meetings. The meeting purpose is to:

1. Lay out the goals and strategies for that day

2. Discuss the expected performance levels for prospect interactions and lead card information

3. Explain to team members exactly how their success is measured at the end of the day

Important in the meeting are a few quick role-plays. Ask each booth worker to give an answer to the typical prospect question of *"so what does your company do?"* Then, see if they reply in a way that is accurate, concise, and clear with your company purpose. You want your attendees to receive a clear, benefit-laden response when they ask about what you do and how you can make their life better.

You can also give attendees the Platinum Rule response. The Platinum Rule response is given when the booth worker identifies the attendee's behavioral style and tailors the answer to meet their needs. When you use a Platinum Rule response, you need to have practiced the pre-determined answers for both direct (Socializer/Director) and indirect (Relater/Thinker) behavioral styles. Keep the response simple and make it easy for your people to respond.

You may also hand out reminder cards to each booth worker that highlight and reinforce your key points from the pre-show training.

The booth worker reminder cards may list:

- Internal product service guides
- Strategies and tactics
- Key points for products
- Key contacts in the company
- Basic booth housekeeping tips
- Primary and secondary competitors
- Booth manners

Do your best to keep the list short and focused. Then, when you have covered your material for the day, close the meetings with an inspirational talk centered on a measurable, daily performance goal.

Compelling Booth Presentations

A presentation at your booth needs to be compelling to the audience, even if your audience is one or one hundred people. The size of the audience is not as important as how simply and effectively you communicate your message. Make sure you tailor your message to your most likely audience,

You also need to compel attendees to take action after viewing "the show." If you do a presentation in your booth, show the audience the benefits from their attendance and make it easy for them to act on the next step in your buying or qualification process.

Also know the reasons why you are giving the presentation. To promote the company's message? Introduce a new product or service? Raise awareness of the company brand or products? Enhance the company image or perception? Move customers along the path to buying your products or services? Generate leads? Qualify leads? You must determine the goals and objectives for giving a presentation, as the presentation is a large investment in time and money.

A compelling booth presentation needs to speak to all four types of behavioral styles. The presentation needs to be closely scripted by the presenter and the supporting cast. Each person needs to know what is expected of him or her, and they need to know when they are supposed to do it.

Use key words and phrases that engage all four of the behavioral styles. Let each person hear something that speaks directly to them. The following is a list of key words and considerations to target the points of your presentations.

Relaters	Socializers
• Discuss teamwork • Highlight safety • Stress harmony • Demonstrate respect for others • Speak warmly and informally	• Present the prestige • Stress the uniqueness • Showcase the fun • Provide testimonials • Present in an enthusiastic manner
Thinkers	**Directors**
• Highlight accuracy • Stress quality • Show reliability • Address obvious disadvantages • Discuss limited risk for failure	• Demonstrate speed • Stress improved results • Give comparable efficiency • Show competitive advantage • Propose specific profit potential

Beyond key words and "hot button" phrases, it is important that the presenter has a high degree of understanding of the company, products, and services, even if the presenter is a hired professional. The presenter must demonstrate competence and interest in their subject matter to be considered credible by the audience. The attendees can easily spot a presenter who does not know their subject matter. But of great importance to the success of the presentation is their delivery, done in Platinum Rule style. A Platinum Rule presentation will speak deep into the hearts and minds of the audience, provided you know their likely behavioral styles and use words and phrases to speak to them.

Make sure to have a third-party person or the Stage Manager hand out and collect survey cards to anyone watching or taking part in a small or large group presentation. Don't leave the survey card job to the presenter. On the card, ask the attendees if they understood the benefits of your products and services. Get their contact information with a promise to give them back a free report, an entry into a drawing, an immediate discount on their first order, etc. Place a call to action on your card. Give the attendee a massive incentive for a limited time, show-only offer. Compile the information you gather, and generate a report to everyone involved in planning and delivering the presentation, telling them how effectively the company achieved the goals of the presentation.

According to Gary Beals, a trade show and sales consultant, information is not nearly as valuable in marketing presentations; to Gary, involvement is the key. Visitors love to participate in demonstrations. With proper planning and the appropriate safety precautions, you may be able to let visitors operate, touch, lift, move, see, hear, or dismantle any and all of the devices or equipment in your display.

If you have a spokesperson, it is always asked if you should you use a microphone for a presentation. If you do, keep the volume level reasonably loud, but not overpowering. This forces anyone who wants to hear you to listen, rather than tune you out from the noise.

If you can, consider *not* using a microphone for your presentations. It will give the presentation a more intimate and human touch, while avoiding a passive listening. It also forces attendees to crowd around the booth area to hear. A crowded booth area will "buzz" with excitement, attracting more attendees as witnesses to the fun.

The exception to the "no microphone rule" is when you use a professional "Infotainer" like Joel Bauer of Bauer and Associates in Chatsworth, Ca. When you have a top professional like Bauer with a proven track record of attracting and motivating crowds to act on your message, then let them monitor their own microphone volume.

We have personally seen Bauer bring in huge crowds to a booth using ear-shattering volume on their P.A. system, simply to overcome the din from surrounding booths and equipment. So be sure to set your volume so that you will be heard without repelling the audience.

Enticing Prospects to "Invade Your Space"

A most overlooked consideration is the "50 foot" rule. The "50 foot" rule states that a prospect should be able to tell from 50 feet away two things.

1.   WHAT you do
2.   HOW you can make their life better or heal their pain

Most every company that you see in an exhibition hall has the name of their company emblazoned all over their booth. And how many times did you have to get within five feet and stand there to decide what they did and how they can make your life better?

Faced with this choice on a busy exhibit floor, most people will choose to walk on by instead of taking their scarce time to unwind the confusion of your booth. Make sure that you minimize your company name, unless you are *very* well branded, and emphasize the "what" in your company, and the problems, solutions, or benefits you offer.

Even if you are very well branded, try to focus on items number one and two because you will not believe how many people do not truly know what you do...until you show them.

Listening to your "Space Invaders"

We may think of listening as being a natural skill requiring no effort beyond the use of our ears. Many of us invest time and money taking classes and seminars in speaking, writing and reading (the "active" communication skills), but how often are we taught the skills of listening?

Actually, effective listening is far from effortless. It is active; and it requires mental processing, hard work and considerable practice. However, the rewards of effective listening can be extremely powerful as it provides the listener with an abundance of information and awareness and, when combined with response adaptability, it creates efficient, satisfying and trusting relationships. Effective listening directly supports The Platinum Rule: the listener accurately hears everything the speaker wants to communicate.

In between your listening, prompt the prospect with good questions to uncover their true needs and motivation to buy. Try to identify as quickly as possible the likely behavioral style of the person, and match pace and directness. Remember that you can quickly identify their style by how direct or indirect they approach you, how open or guarded they answer your questions. Also know a few basic Platinum Rule strategies to use during your conversation, allowing the other person to feel comfortable during their time in your booth.

Consider the following table as a guide to use, and incorporate this knowledge as part of your pre-show booth worker training and role-play.

Direct and Open	Indirect and Open
Socializer	*Relater*
• Show enthusiasm	• Talk warmly and informally
• Let them set the pace	• Explore their needs
• Explore their motivations and big ideas	• Emphasize harmony and teamwork
• Balance questions with personal stories	• Ask their feelings about the talk
• Provide testimonials	• Respect their position
• Emphasize uniqueness and prestige	• Provide them personal assurance

Direct and Guarded	Indirect and Guarded
Director • Move and speak fast • Get to the point quickly • Learn their time constraints • Stress benefits • Emphasize results • Give a quick analysis with 2-3 choices	*Thinker* • Avoid social talk • Focus on the facts and details • Emphasize accuracy and quality • Use short, fact-oriented questions • Let them speak of their expertise • Ask if they have concerns

Don't allow the prospect leave your booth without learning as much as you can about them. Give your business development and sales people a head start in the lead development process. To do so, hone your skills to the point that you have to disengage most prospects on your time, not theirs. Let them want to stay in your area because you know how to listen, and listen in a way that feels most comfortable to their natural style.

Plant Seeds During the Show

When you are a great listener, you build a quick trust and bond with the prospects. The trust will allow you to present one or two key benefits to compel them to think about you and your company long after the show is over.

Remember, there are many other "farmers" out there planting seeds with your prospects and customers during a show, but you want to be the one who is remembered by how you treated that person according to their natural behavioral style. Of course your flawless follow-up will be the water that gets the seed to grow, but realize that for both the Thinker and Relater styles, planting seeds is about all you should expect from a meeting at the show.

Save Trees; Leave Your Brochures Home

Do you know that 82% of literature never gets back to the office? Make it a point to not give away literature at shows, but instead promise to mail the specific pack in less than one week following a show.

Will you have show giveaways? Why? Something? Nothing? What are the giveaways and what is the message and purpose of the giveaway? DOES THE GIVEAWAY HAVE A LONG-TERM, LEGITIMATE USE FOR THE ATTENDEE, BEYOND A FEW DAYS AFTER THE SHOW? What is the cost?

Don't get caught up in the "everyone's doing it" mentality of handing out sales brochures and literature at a show. Instead give a small, pocket-sized giveaway of the "How To" or "10 Tips" format that will have your logo and helpful information. Give them help that they will save for future reference, and make sure that the giveaway is written in the style of your most likely target audience.

A very important tip is to place a sticker or a stamp on your brochures that shows the show name, dates, and location on the front or the back. Of the few brochures and information kept by attendees, you need to give them a chance to remember where they found you. This memory jogger is especially helpful during lead development after the show. The prospect needs to know where they met you and can use their memories to move the sales or relationship process forward, not back to square one.

Another good tip is to have a space where the booth worker or salesperson can write their name and phone number on the giveaway. A great chance to start the person-to-person relationship and give the prospect a direct contact with a name and face they trust.

The Power of Great Lead Forms

The lead form is the sheet or card used by your booth staffers to document their conversations with prospects and customers. However, it is not an interrogation sheet. The lead form should be used to guide, not dictate, the flow and topics of the conversation. Don't rely on your lead form as a script that must be followed to the letter. Allow the conversation with the prospect and customer to flow and be guided from the questions on the lead form.

A common approach to capture attendee information is to use electronic lead gathering. However, this form of lead gathering does not capture much personal information beyond the contact information from the show association. So look to your program and see if you gather leads by indiscriminately scanning the attendee badges. In most cases there is nothing wrong with using electronic data collection as a backup, but do you want the Show Association to have your prospect lists from the card reader?

As a way to leverage the valuable face-to-face time with the attendee, have your team use a well-designed Platinum Rule based lead form. The lead form is the link between the show and the Business Development group to move forward the sales and marketing process in the weeks and months following the show.

The Lead Form is very, very important!

Have a formal lead form and use it! Train your booth workers prior to the show in the method of going through the form. Determine if the prospect meets your qualifications and where they are in the buying cycle.

Try to identify the "information gatherers" as quickly as possible in order to disqualify them. However, before you leave the "information gatherer," try to get them to tell you the name of the person or contact at their company who has the authority or interest in your product.

Ask if they are at the show, and if they arrive, remember their name and company and greet them as if you had personally invited them to your booth.

During lead collection, collect as much specific information about the prospect as possible. The information includes their interests in yours and other areas, and their buying timetable or cycle. What is their specific purpose in attending the trade show? Are there other complementary goods or services that could help them?

Make sure you also learn the timetable of any particular projects, any and all of the decision makers involved, and whether or not budgets have been written for the project.

Are there any other companies already with proposals submitted? If so, you must make yours so dramatically different in your proposed solution that the prospective customer will have to take a hard look at yours. Without the ability to "change the game," your proposal will most likely be a justification of their previous decision to buy from your competitor.

Lead Form Example

Your booth staffers should be the only people to fill out the lead form. Give the people with the face-to-face interaction the responsibility to gather the information you need to conduct a productive and meaningful follow-up. When you have a prospect that takes time to meet with you, use the time during your 3-5 minutes together to fill out the lead form card as the conversation allows. We know you will not be expected to get answers to all of your questions, but let the flow of the questions allow the prospect to open up to you and get them to talk and reveal their true motivations, interests, or curiosities.

A Platinum Rule lead form follows. The card can and should be modified to suit the specifics of a particular show, completed 4-6 weeks in advance of the show by the Stage Manager, approved by your trade show team, and used with each and every interaction you have with attendees.

Sample Platinum Rule Lead Form

1. Why are you at the Show?

    ☐ New Technology   ☐ Buy Products

    ☐ Save Money   ☐ See Customers

    ☐ See Vendors   ☐ Other

2. Currently use our products? ☐ Yes ☐ No

    Previous user? ☐ Yes ☐ No

3. Which Products? _____

    _____

    _____

    _____

    _____

4. Currently doing:

    ☐ Consulting   ☐ Direct Marketing

    ☐ Motivational Seminars   ☐ Public Speaking

5. Most Likely Style:

    ☐ Relater   ☐ Thinker

    ☐ Socializer   ☐ Director

6.　　☐ Indirect　　　☐ Direct

　　　　☐ Slow　　　　☐ Fast

7. Considering a change of Suppliers?　☐ Yes　☐ No

Why?

_____

_____

_____

_____

_____

8. Are you:　　☐ Getting into any new areas, or

　　　　　　　☐ Expanding your current business?

9. What is your timeline to purchase?

_____

10. Other companies quoting?

_____

11. Is this project currently budgeted?　☐ Yes　☐ No

12. Approximate budget amount.

_____

13. What are the 2 or 3 things most important to you
when choosing a supplier?

_____

_____

_____

_____

_____

14. May we have permission to stay in touch? ☐ Yes ☐ No

15. May I contact you for the follow-up? ☐ Yes ☐ No

16. Others involved in decisions: _____

_____

_____

_____

_____

17.   How to contact the others involved in decision?
         ☐ Phone ☐ Fax ☐ Email ☐ Personal Visits

_____

18.   Best ways to stay in touch with attendee:
         ☐ Phone ☐ Fax ☐ Email ☐ Personal Visits

_____

19.   Easiest way to help you learn about our company and products: _____

_____

_____

_____

20. Competitive Influences/Who is Current Supplier

_____

_____

21. Additional thoughts/information

_____

_____

At the end of the discussion with the prospect/suspect/customer, return the completed lead card with their contact information to the Stage Manager. Then be ready to engage another prospect and ask good questions and listen once again. Don't try to sell at the booth unless the prospect tells you they are ready for a bid right now!

Time is on your side and will be used by Business Development to grow the seeds you plant in the minds of the prospects at the show.

PROFILING PROSPECTS:
Beyond Card Swiping

There is a growing trend with exhibiting companies using the automated kiosks or screens to gather information on a prospect. However, people remember people, and your best bet for quality information is a face-to-face meeting that leads to an initial impression of you and your company. The "and" of the info gathering equation could be a person-to-person interaction with a booth staffer, using a lead form card, followed by a brief, concluding kiosk survey.

However, some companies insist on exclusively using the automated kiosks, so if your company has the budget to rent or purchase these machines, use the opportunity to build the list of questions in the machine with Platinum Rules in mind.

Make sure that the first question on the screen gets the prospect to *indirectly* identify their primary behavioral style by a list of questions. The easiest way to do this is to ask them questions that let them tell you how they buy expensive items (slow or fast) and what they want at work (harmony or results). Depending on how they answer, you will know if they are direct or indirect, open or guarded. That will profile their natural style and your questions can then take into consideration a Platinum Rule based approach, similar to the approaches given in Section One of this book, and the table given in the *"Compelling Booth Presentations"* chapter of this section.

Generically, you can structure your kiosk interview to ask the prospect if they prefer their information to include facts, data, and technical specs, or if they prefer their information to stress the outcomes, timelines, benefits, and payouts. Just knowing the type of information they prefer will let you know if they are either a Director or Socializer vs. a Relater or Thinker. The ones who prefer the facts and data are the Relater/Thinker types, and the ones who prefer the outcomes and benefits are the Director/Socializer types.

Next, you need to structure your questions to speak to the different styles, again using the information from the table in *"Compelling Booth Presentations"* as well as the table information from *"Listening to Your Space Invaders."* You ask the person questions that speak to their basic desire for outcome, whether it is inclusion, results, profits, details, improvements, or even enjoyment. You can get a better idea of the truth behind the person's real needs when you ask questions that speak directly to their behavioral style.

Initial impressions are lasting, so interact personally and helpfully and leverage that first impression opportunity in your favor.

HAVE FUN ON STAGE:
Adapt Your Platinum Style on the Show Floor

A key to any successful show program is the ability to adapt to your surroundings and situations, and to make adjustments "on the fly." Not always do things go as planned, and when they don't, you have to be able to find the opportunity within the problem.

In this section, we discuss how you can use Platinum Rules to adapt to most any situation. And when you are in a situation such as Ric Wiley of Tri-Power, Inc. in Akron, Ohio, you find the way to not only adapt but to thrive.

Working at the Great Lakes Industrial Show, Ric's booth was in the aisle across from the Ridgid Tool booth. For years, Ridgid Tool had an annual "tool calendar" that featured female models in bathing suits, each brandishing a Ridgid Tool. At the Great Lakes Show, the Ridgid bathing suit models were in the booth, signing calendars and drawing huge crowds.

The aisles were blocked for 50 feet in all directions as fans waited to get their signed calendars. Unfortunately, the views of the adjacent booths were also blocked. Rather than get upset about the situation, the Tri-Power booth took the opportunity to engage the captive audience as they waited in line. They took the blocked aisles and treated them as their own private focus group; asking questions, qualifying, beginning great relationships.

As a result of using their abilities to adapt to the situation and get personal with the lines of prospects blocking the aisles, they experienced an increase of over 53% in qualified leads from the previous show, with a corresponding increase in sales over the coming year. That is why you can use your knowledge of The Platinum Rule and be able to make the best of most any situation.

Smooth Conversations using Behavioral Adaptability

Effectively adapting your style meets the key expectations of others in specific situations... whether in personal or business relationships. Through attention and practice, you can achieve higher adaptability levels and recognize when it is necessary to adapt to the other person's behavioral style.

As you develop your adaptability to more effectively deal with the other person's expectations and tendencies, you automatically decrease tension and increase trust. This enables you to interact more positively with all people... including customers you may have previously lost due to a conflict in selling/buying styles. You will ease strained situations while establishing rapport and credibility. Your ability to adapt your style will make the difference between harmonious, productive relationships or friction-filled encounters with others.

Make Friends from Strangers

Once you understand your own primary style and the style of the person you want to build rapport with, you can begin to adapt your style. Your first adaptations should be *pace* and *priority*. By making simple adjustments in your speed of operation and your focus on tasks or relationships, you can eliminate a lot of relationship "static." Remember that changing your style takes time, practice and patience. Life is a journey, not a quick fix. This is why you should refer back to this book often and consider every human interaction a wonderful opportunity to practice your adaptation skills.

Adjust Your Pace

If you are a direct person, you tend to operate at a fast rate. If you want to connect with an indirect person, you will want to talk, walk and make decisions with them more slowly. The easiest way to slow down is to take a deep breath, relax, and invite the other person to lead the conversation and share in the decision-making process. If you follow their lead rather than trying to take control, the pace is dictated by the person who matters most; your prospect or customer!

Be sure to engage in active listening to ensure that you thoroughly understand what the other person is saying. Resist your impulses to interrupt. Listen more than you talk. Avoid the impulse to criticize, challenge or push the communication along faster than the other person wants to go. Try to find points of agreement, but if you do disagree, choose your words carefully and do not intimidate the indirect person.

If you are an indirect person, you tend to operate at a slower speed. In dealing with a direct person, you will want to talk, walk and make decisions with them more rapidly. Ask your questions and give your answers with short, concise responses. Don't drag out conversations with a laundry list of details and your personal experience and interpretations. Let the other person give their experience and interpretations.

It is helpful to initiate conversations and give recommendations, but don't force your will on the other person. Communicate with a strong, confident voice and maintain eye contact. If you disagree with the person, do not make an argument out of the point. However, if you have to say something to correct a fact, express the fact confidently but tactfully. Again, avoid your opinions. Face the situation openly without turning it into conflict or a personal attack.

Adjust Your Priority

If you are an open person, relationships and feelings primarily motivate you; they are your top priority. If you are dealing with a guarded person, you must make a behavioral adjustment. Increase your task-oriented focus by getting right to the agenda. Talk about and focus on the bottom line of the project at hand. The person you are dealing with will want logic and facts, so be prepared to provide proof of your rationale with supporting information.

Guarded people do not like to be touched by strangers or to have their physical space invaded. Do not initiate physical contact until you are sure it will be positively received. Dress and speak in a professional manner compatible with the successful people in your industry. A guarded person needs to trust and respect you and your credibility. Initiate physical contact and try standing a little closer than your normal style might dictate. Use a few relaxed gestures like leaning back, smiling, or gently patting the other person on the back or shoulder.

Easy Booth Strategies by Behavioral Type

With Directors: Be Efficient and Competent

When adapting your style to a Director, it is important to acknowledge their priorities and objectives. Learn which goals are most important to them and then let them know how you can be an asset for helping them achieve each one. Be professional, competent and businesslike. Get down to business immediately. Be punctual (if not early) to the appointment, have a prepared agenda and stick to it! If you find yourself running late to the meeting, be sure to call ahead and explain the facts behind your reason for tardiness.

If you disagree with them, keep your objections based on facts, not personal feelings. Recognize their ideas and achievements rather than them personally.

Directors want to know what your product or service does, the time involved and what it will cost. They are interested in saving time, results, increasing profitability, forward progress and gaining any edge over competition.

With Socializers: Be Interested in Them

When adapting to a Socializer, support their opinions, ideas and dreams. Find out what they are trying to accomplish and let them know how you can support them. Do not hurry the discussion and allow them to discuss sideline issues or personal interests. Be entertaining, fun and fast moving, but do it without removing the spotlight from them.

Make sure the Socializer understands exactly what to expect from you and your product or service. Summarize who is to do what, where and when. Minimize arguments and conflict. Use testimonials and incentives to influence the decision process in a positive manner. Illustrate your ideas with stories and emotional descriptions that they can relate to their goals or interests.

Socializers are interested in knowing how your product or service will enhance their status and visibility. They are interested in saving effort, so make the process easy for them. Once they make a decision, they do not want to be bothered with paperwork, installation, training or service problems. Clearly summarize details for them and direct them towards mutually agreeable objectives.

With Thinkers: Be Thorough and Well-Prepared

Adapting to a Thinker requires careful, well-prepared support for their organized, thoughtful approach. Greet them cordially, but then proceed quickly to the task without spending time with small talk. Demonstrate your commitment and sincerity through your actions rather than words or promises. Be systematic, precise and provide solid, tangible, factual evidence of the benefit of your product or service. Be prepared to answer the detailed questions that Thinkers ask.

Thinkers love charts, graphs and analyses that boil a lot of information down into a concise format. Back your proposal with guarantees that substantially reduce their risks. The closer you can come to a risk-free decision, the more likely you are to get an approval decision from a Thinker.

Thinkers want to know how your product or service works and how they can justify it logically. They are risk avoiders; their greatest fear is that they will be embarrassed by a poor decision or action. Provide them with enough data and documentation to prove the value of your proposal. Give them time to think and make their choice; avoid pushing them into a hasty decision.

With Relaters: Be Warm and Sincere

Adapt to Relaters by being personally interested in them. Find out about their background, their family and their interests, and share similar information about yourself. Allow them time to develop confidence in you and move along in an informal, slow manner. Encourage them to get other interested parties involved in the decision-making process (since they will anyway).

Assume that they will take everything personally and minimize disagreements and conflict. Practice your active listening skills, be sure to take notes and display your commitment to them and their objectives. Provide guarantees and your personal assurances that any decisions they make will involve a minimum of risk. Let them know how your organization works and how it stands behind your products and services.

Relaters want to know how your product or service will affect their personal circumstances. Save them any possible embarrassment by making sure all the interested parties and decision makers are involved with the sales process from the beginning. Keep the Relater involved and emphasize the human element of your product or service. Communicate with them in a consistent manner on a regular basis.

Build Rapport and Connect with Prospects Before they leave

A very effective and easy way to build rapport with a prospect is to use the "please tell me about" line of questions during your time spent together. Even the most impatient Director will always spend at least 30 seconds with you when you ask them to tell you something about themselves.

We have found that when you ask a prospect to tell you something about where they are from (as listed on their badge), and interject a personal experience you may have with their area (landmarks, celebrities, and cuisine of the region always make great discussion), you then let the other person be the expert on the subject.

Even if you ask them to explain to you either what makes them stand out in their job, or what are the one or two best kept secrets about their company, a prospect will usually speak to you with pride and animation. They will transform from a defensive posture, waiting to be sold, to a relaxed posture that one gets when they find a "friend" that is willing to listen to them.

Everyone is an expert in something. Do your best to find out what they consider themselves "expert" in, and then stand back and learn something! You will develop a rapport and connection with that prospect which makes your Platinum-style lead development transition faster into an opportunity to do business.

Disengage with a Platinum Promise

When you have a Business Development group in place to process your show leads, you have the ability to use a systematic approach to developing a lead for weeks, months, and years after the show. With a backup in place, you may relate to the prospect the promise to provide them with more helpful information beyond your brief meeting on the show floor.

However, the key to this promise is making it with their behavioral style in mind. You should make the promise of results to the Director, the promise of detailed information to the Thinker, the promise of a fun experience to the Socializer, and the promise of working with your team to the Relater.

Most companies promise many things while on the show floor, and usually each promise is based on a sales pitch. When a company presents a promise to a prospect that speaks directly to their basic style as a human being, and is implemented by a systematic approach that continues to feed their primary style, the likelihood of conversion to customer will increase dramatically.

AT THE INTERMISSION:
Improve Your Platinum Plan with Feedback

When you work a show at the booth level, you want to know how others see you, and the overall effect of your marketing and people at the show. Although it takes time and manpower to do an exit interview, you need to know the impression and experience that your attendees have when they leave your booth. To accomplish this, a staffer, preferably one not associated with your staff, needs to sample attendees as they leave your booth and travel to the ends of the aisles. You really need both short and long-term feedback to make adjustments during the course of the show, and to make the wholesale changes to your booth, staff, and messages over time.

It is not intrusive to have prepared 4-6 short questions to ask the attendee after they have left your booth. You would want to know:

1. How would they rate their overall experience on a 1-10 scale and why?

2. What do they believe your company does?

3. How does your company help others?

4.   The quality of your staff.

5.   The impression of your booth.

6.   The likelihood they would ever do business with you and why or why not.

Again, you want to know. Especially if you have your messages targeting a particular set of behavioral styles, and for some reason you missed the mark and did not know it. That is where you can make a change during the course of the show and get back to communicating to your target audience.

Remember, Kinko's is always open, so don't be afraid to have a few new signs or banners made if your messages have missed the mark!

Listen to your staff

This point is obvious, and probably the most overlooked by exhibit managers. Your foot soldiers are the ones your trust on the front lines to be the ambassadors for your company. Now we are not talking about you bending to every suggestions and critique offered by a staffer, but know that your people can tell if your plan and approach is working.

If the staff has "buy-in," meaning they have participated in some of the aspects of the show plan, they will usually want to contribute to the betterment and success of the group. Especially when you have Directors and Socializers as part of the mix. The Thinkers and Relaters will let you know another way, usually after the show, but for those and the rest of your staff, you should have in place a feedback mechanism for the staff to show you what works and doesn't work. Also, remember to listen to not just "what" they say, but "how" they say it if you have a way to interview or capture their feedback beyond a multiple choice setting.

Let your people know that well-thought, intelligent feedback will always be taken seriously. Also let them know that feedback in the form of never-ending complaints will not be taken at all! So for every the daily debriefing and strategy session before you move on to the enjoyment of the evening.

4) If you don't have an answer to the toughest question(s), then get them before the next day of the show. At your pre-show meeting and briefing, share the answers with your people. The best way to present them is written on a sheet or a card. Practice a quick role play before the show opens. Get your people comfortable with responding to the tough questions.

5) If you need to change your plan, in most cases the changes will be small, not major overhauls. The small changes could be the addition or subtraction of a question on the booth card, or a message on a sign or demo. Either way, don't be afraid to make changes while still at the show, and give yourself time to try out the new approach while the matter is still fresh to you and the staff.

6) If major changes are needed, then do them! If you are going to spend additional days at the show working a flawed plan, then take the time to make the changes that will turn around a potentially bad show plan and make it workable or brilliant while at the show.

7) It is always a great idea to have a Plan B and even a Plan C available to you at a moment's notice. The elements of the backup plan should be in place before you ever attend the show, with a person or persons responsible for making the call to change each and every day.

8) The ability to be flexible and adaptable on the show floor will make the difference between exceeding or falling short of your show goals, so plan for the unknown, and leave the helpless feelings to the people in the booth next door!

point of feedback, make sure you get a corresponding solution from the staffer, and bring about the best feedback and solutions to your team for discussion.

During the discussion, try not to let the Directors and Socializers dominate the conversation. If many of the feedback items are given by the less-direct part of your team, they may believe that they are being "shouted down." So give each person equal voice and time, but most of all foster an environment where all styles believe they can give feedback in a way that is taken seriously.

Why Wait? Improve Your Plan Each Day

Again, Doug MacLean of MacLean Marketing offers valuable contribution to this section. This section is the most popular part of his consulting business; making mid-course corrections at the booth to reach target goals at the show. These course corrections may happen each day at the show. Before each day of the show, Doug teaches his clients their purpose is to gather, assess, evaluate, adjust, and GO to reach pre-show targets. So why not take this approach for each and every day of the show? The following is a summary of Doug's best practices.

1) Instead of each person running off to do their own agenda for the evening, do your best to keep the group together for a few minutes after the show closes, and have a quick, pre-defined series of checkmarks and questions to answer before or during dinner.

2) Before the show starts, let your booth staff know the list of questions you will ask them at the close of the show that day. Have the staff thinking, planning, and documenting the answers to the information you will require.

3) Ask which question(s) worked best, what points of the interaction did they like/dislike, what product was liked/ disliked the best, the best question they were asked, the best answer they gave, the toughest question not answered etc. Have

A Different Stage is Better

An effective approach used by the best companies is to make their booths flexible not only from show to show, but from day to day, and in some cases, hour to hour.

Why make your stage different? Because it catches the attention of prospects, even if they do not know how or why the stage is different. You may have a prospect that walks right by your booth on the first or second day of the show, maybe even the morning of the first day, and does not stop. If you present a different layout, or lighting, or signage that may speak to their style (try Direct approach signage the first day and Indirect the second), they then may stop.

Putting out the Direct and Indirect signage in the same show may be fun and interesting, but your best success should come when you know the likely styles of your attendees in advance, and cater your messages to them. If you know that your likely audience is Directors and Thinkers, then you need to have the messages that speak in results and details. This is possible, even though the requirements of both styles are so different.

You also want to have a different stage if you have many shows and the same staff working each show. Mix it up for them, do not let them get into a rut! People re-arrange their offices to generate a new motivation from the old routine, and show stages are the same way. Give it a different layout, look, or feel and monitor the results for future evaluation and use.

And by all means, tell "what" you do, and "how" you make the attendee's life better. Let the attendee be able to know something more about you than your name from 50 feet away. It helps them to decide if they need to stop and explore further, or to move on. At the very least, it saves your staff from many of the "so what do you do?" questions from unqualified prospects.

Management Feedback Matters

Management is the group that has the power to build or retreat your budgets. If you include your management in your decision-making, you have the opportunity to bring the successes and failures of your program to light as early as possible. Then, the faster you can bring about either a plan to build on success, or turn around poor habits or performance, the better your overall plan will be.

Many companies have their management detached from their show programs, especially in the larger operations with at least one or more shows per month. However, it is the feedback from management that will give you insight into areas that you can use to improve or expand.

A simple survey to your management will give you as the exhibits manager an insight into the impressions and desires of your management. Use this survey to uncover their starting point, and then build on the strengths and improve the weaknesses.

To each manager responsible for budgets and personnel in your show program, ask:

1.   What was the most successful trade show you ever exhibited, and why?

2.   What was the worst show you ever exhibited, and why?

3.   How long does it usually take to build a relationship with a prospect before they switch to you and start buying from you?

4.   What will happen to the leads you generate from this show?

5.   What accountability is there for the people given the leads from this show?

6.   What system(s) do they use to stay on top of the leads, even if it takes many months or years to get a sale?

7.   What happened to the leads you got at trade shows you did a year or more ago?

8.   How do you measure the success or failure of a trade show?

9.   How can you tell if a trade show is profitable?

10.   Is your trade show plan designed to attract and convert specific types of prospects?

Most managers will find these questions to be provocative and revealing to the potential opportunities and challenges of your show program. It is our opinion that you be ready with an action plan to account for every question, or at least an intelligent response.

Bring the reality of your current show program to light, and start working on filling the holes with the support, not the scorn, of your management.

The Court of Public Opinion

There is information you need to know about prospects in general, and it revolves around their general opinions. Specific opinions about you and your products/services/booth will come around during the exit interviews, but know from each and every show the answers to the following:

1.   Are you typically attending the show to buy, or do you come to the show for other reasons? If for other reasons, what are they?

2.   How far in the future do you begin planning and evaluating major and complex purchases?

3.   One or two months after attending a trade show, how much do you typically remember about a product, a company, a booth, or a salesperson?

4.   If you remember something, what is it that makes you remember?

5.   What percentage of companies or salespeople follows up with you after the trade show when you give them your card or scan your information?

6.   How long do most salespeople stay in touch with you while you are still a prospect and not a customer?

7.   What percentage of salespeople asks you how and when you would like them to follow up with you?

8.   When you make a purchase, do you put more emphasis on the trust you have with the salesperson or the reputation or trust of the company?

9.   How might a good salesperson build trust with you?

10.   How do you like to be treated by someone working the booth?

Knowing the answers to these questions will give you the information you need to create a great overall plan that you can build on for the future of your exhibit operations.

THE CURTAIN FALLS:

Deliver the Encore for Great Results

When the trade show is over and your role as entertainer ends, the next stage in the process of trade show mastery is the development of leads into customers. In reality, your role changes from entertainer to farmer. Consider your new leads as being the seeds to tremendous future business. You want to reap a crop of new customers with these leads serving as your seeds.

However, like any good farmer, you must cultivate and grow the seeds into a future harvest. This is where most companies fail in their efforts to show a return on their trade show investment. If you company can purchase and implement a "Lead Farm", you will be able to outsell and outgrow your competition in the months and years following the show.

During the encore is when you switch your thoughts from being the helpful entertainer to being the helpful and consistent farmer. In this section, we show you the ways to both think and act when cultivating and growing your leads into customers. Follow this plan and watch your collection of "seeds" from the show grow into large harvests of new customers in the months and years following the fall of the show curtain.

Post-Show Success is like Growing Tomatoes

When you send a direct mail, email, etc. to a prospect or customer, push for or ask for permission for an action step. In essence, action to send for more information, a free sample, a free analysis, a follow-up call. This gives you the opportunity to further qualify a prospect; you can concentrate on a larger presentation of the features, benefits, and applications of your product or service.

Give your prospects many opportunities to show their interest. Understand that your prospect or target market may miss the message the first time it is sent. Even if the message is "targeted" through a Relationship (sniper) based campaign. Give a prospect multiple opportunities to say "yes" to your offer. Do not stop at one, two, or even three attempts. Segment your marketing into four or more smaller bites, as this increases your chance at getting noticed and educating the prospect without overwhelming them.

To better qualify your leads or prospects, ask them to fill out or fill in a few lines of information on their reply to your marketing. You raise the quality of the lead response. Do not ask them to check off a box on a reply card.

When you script a series of follow-ups from a trade show, or for a marketing campaign, make your messages and offers different for each level of decision-maker you reach. The message and offer you submit to an engineer will be different than for a marketing manager, and different than for a CEO. Understand what motivates a particular decision maker to action and structure your message and offerings to speak to these motivating factors.

Know what motivates your decision maker. Higher-level executives find value with items that save time or buy them time, rather than save them a few dollars. Middle managers will like safe and time-tested products or services, in order to preserve their jobs. Engineers will like cutting-edge, high-productivity items. Tailor your marketing efforts to these tendencies and you will achieve a higher response.

When you respond to a trade show lead, or court a prospect, consider using a testimonial or case history. If you are a large company, show a testimonial or case history that depicts your ability to provide fast and personal service. If you are a small company, show something that showcases your strength and stability. Finally, for all customers, show in your testimonials how seeking more information while they were in the prospect stage rewarded the end user.

If you doubt how your message will be received, then play it safe and use more formal language and benefits statements. Do not attempt to be humorous or cute if you are in doubt.

If you are exhibiting a new product or service at a trade show, understand that your follow-up campaign must be education-oriented, and staggered over a series of timely "drips." It will take more time and effort for you to get an appointment, so pre-plan a series of personalized, scripted follow-ups that target the level of decision maker and educate them in terms they will understand.

When you script an email follow-up campaign for a series of leads, ask the recipient to forward the email to other people in their company. If you send out a direct-mail campaign, then include a second-response medium with it. It will increase your response rates without significantly raising your campaign costs.

When you send a mailing, or even an email to a top executive, understand an executive assistant may screen your marketing. If you can learn the name of the executive assistant, send your marketing to them, with a note outlining the importance of the top executive reading your message.

The next step is to get your friend to be your customer. A friend will only become your customer when you build your relationship on a foundation that addresses a need that is sometimes very personal to them. The prospect need you address can only become a sale when the friend has the budget and timetable to buy from you. Don't worry if the time to buy takes months, or even years!

When your "friend" finally becomes a customer, the sales professional realizes that the job has merely begun. The steps to obtain the customer must be continued to keep the customer and build repeat business.

Getting more results (business) from your trade show leads is a dedicated, systematic process. You must integrate technology with personal and targeted messages that get your prospect to pay attention to you, and ultimately listen to your value proposition.

In this age of impersonal, generic marketing, you will win by establishing a "personal" relationship with your prospects that shows them you are truly interested in their needs, and offer a solution to the "pain" in their life. Take the time to divide your offerings into small, bite-sized portions, and keep the information coming to your prospect over the length of their buying cycle.

You will be amazed at the positive response, and your bottom line will improve from your trade show efforts.

Lead Follow-up Using a System

There are three distinct benefits to implementing and executing a Lead Management System. The first is an increase in sales opportunities immediately after the show. Hot prospects no longer fall through the cracks. The second is a greater conversion for your leads that have long buying cycles. Long-term leads are no longer thrown away. The third is the ability to measure results to determine effectiveness, and make adjustments to future show plans and post-show marketing efforts.

Think about your prospect. A prospect will not listen to your value proposition until they trust you. How many times do you follow up a trade show lead, only to hear, "Who are you, what does your company do, I don't remember you from the show?"

According to Ruth Stevens, direct marketing expert and author of _Trade Show and Event Marketing,_ "_the secret to success in business to business is in the process. It's not about marketing creativity. The leverage lies in converting more inquiries into qualified leads, then more qualified leads into sales...in short, the company with the best lead management is the one that will win._"

You must have a business process that touches the prospect at least three or four times in a meaningful way, after the show, before you make the first phone call. Use a combination of emails, handwritten cards, and SPECIFIC information to their inquiry, not your full-line catalog.

Have your sales team make the first phone call after the initial "touches" have been sent. At that time, the prospect will know more about you and your company, and the sales process will move forward, not start over.

Profile the prospect based on their needs, position, and personality if possible. Ask their PERMISSION to continue to send them relevant and informative items beyond your call. Attempt to determine a timetable for their purchase, and then execute a series of timely follow-ups based on their expressed interests.

The secret to sales after a trade show does indeed lie in the process. Have your company subscribe to a service that will touch your prospects for you, or set up a business development program that will execute and track the prospects, over months or years if necessary.

A touch program of meaningful information, i.e. saying to the prospect *"here's another great reason to come back and do business with our company,"* will build trust with them. Then, when the lead is developed and high in the buying cycle, you can turn over the lead to sales as a qualified, hot lead, and let them do what they do best...make the sale and build your business.

Pull the Weeds (Qualify and Profile)

When you look at your best customers, try to think of how they made your "A" list. Did they start out as a great customer, or did you court them, almost like a relationship, to build the trust that helped them listen to you and realize the value of doing business with you?

Your Sales Team needs to know the answers to the following to be effective:

1. Is the prospect now or tomorrow in your business?
2. Is the prospect going to buy something in the future? (Your products or services)
3. When is the purchase considered? (Timetable)
4. Is there an approximate or approved budget for the project?
5. Who are the decision makers for the buying decision?

Don't confuse need vs. timing. Is the prospect the type that will buy one machine in the next year, or the type that will buy 20 machines within three years? Ask the prospect "will you ever need, or will you ever buy what we have?"

Is your prospect cycle a transactional cycle (ready to buy now) or a relationship cycle (will eventually buy from someone)? Know what the prospect must go through before they will buy from you, and make it happen!

Tailor your first post-show contacts to warm, inform, and determine the time frame of the prospect's needs. Then, move the qualified leads into a program that either accelerates the sales process for hot leads, or builds trust and relationships with prospects having long-term buying cycles. Ask permission to stay in touch, and provide timely, relevant information that is expected and anticipated. Cut through the attention deficit that most prospects have during their busy day.

Most salespeople do not have the time or interest to administer a "trust-building" program, so great companies will employ a system or service to do this for them. Look to develop, purchase, or subscribe to a system that allows a pre-scripting and automatic sending of targeted messages and mailings. Send messages OVER TIME on behalf of your salesperson.

Automatically sending the right messages over time builds trust and lets the salesperson concentrate instead on closing the current "hot" sales opportunities. Make sure to have your system send reminders to the salesperson on the day information is sent, outlining what was sent on their behalf. That way, should they receive a call from the prospect, they will know why they were contacted.

A system to periodically "touch" your prospect with useful information will build top-of-mind awareness and let the prospect know you care about building a relationship. In _What Clients Love,_ Harry Beckwith states that companies have long-term relationships based on "comfort" with their supplier. Are your prospects and clients comfortable with you?

You Can't Rush the Harvest

When you know the four behavior styles of a buyer using The Platinum Rule, you should then tailor your follow-up to match the style or styles of prospect they represent.

According to Michael Bosworth in his book *Solution Selling*, your prospects will have four typical responses to your sales efforts. The following paragraphs list the four common responses to sales efforts from prospects, and the true meaning of the response.

The first response given to your sales efforts, although implicitly, is that the prospect does not truly understand your product or service. Most prospects will not readily admit this situation to you, and choose to quickly dismiss your sales efforts. It is easier for them to reject or ignore your sales efforts than to admit they do not understand the value of your product or service.

The second response is that the prospect never uses your product or service. These leads probably should not have been gathered in the first place. Consider changing your booth and advertising to clarify your message and avoid attracting these prospects in the future.

The third response is that the prospect uses your products and services, and is currently getting these products and services from another company. THESE ARE YOUR BEST PROSPECTS! If you position yourself as the second source, you will be ready when the first source stumbles or takes the relationship for granted.

The fourth response is the "We are looking to buy now, please send a salesperson right away!" BE VERY WARY OF THESE PROSPECTS, THEY USUALLY HAVE THEIR SOLUTION BUILT WITH ANOTHER COMPANY AND WILL USE YOU TO JUSTIFY THEIR PREVIOUS DECISION. Your only chance here is if you can re-engineer the solution to position your company as the only one to satisfy the need or eliminate the "pain." (Another gem from *Solution Selling*)

Water the Leads

Consider the situation of the prospect. They attend a show or fill out a response card in hopes of receiving information. For weeks after the show or mailer, they are bombarded with impersonal general catalogs and flyers, which may or may not pertain to their interests. Then, their voice mail is filled with follow-up messages from salespeople they do not know. The prospect might not remember you or your company in this information barrage. Then, the salesperson's follow-up phone calls are like a cold-call, a re-introduction of your company. As a result, the phone calls are usually brief. ("*Please send me your information and I will look at it.*")

The sales effort is usually geared to "harvest" a quick sale. **A prospect will not listen to your value proposition until they know and trust you!** As a result, your salespeople quickly become discouraged with the prospect, and the lead is discarded or entered into a "dead file" or the trash can, never again to see the light of day.

To understand this reality, we should look at how we sell. At this point, know that traditional sales efforts are backwards. This is important to understand. Salespeople first attempt to get the sale, then to build trust. It should be the other way around. Build the trust **FIRST**. According to Harry Beckwith in *What Clients Love* the best salespeople sell in this order:

1.   Themselves

2.   Their Company

3.   Their Product or Service

4.   Their Price

Therefore, when the prospect knows you, then trusts you, they are willing to listen to your value proposition. You can then work on generating a sale because your true value to them will be heard. It does not matter if you have the best widget or service in the world, if your message is not absorbed by the prospect, you will not have a chance to get the sale.

Sell a Corkscrew, Not a Swiss Army Knife

Prospects are often confused by sales giving them too much general product information during and after a show (like a Swiss army knife). Learn how to find a specific area of "pain" in the prospect's life, and propose a solution specific to their need (the corkscrew) with one or two products or services. Build your relationship with a prospect around one specific product or service to get your foot in the door before you up-sell or cross-sell other items.

For example: Does a restaurant menu with 10 pages seem confusing? Would you make a faster and easier choice if the menu were limited to one or two pages? Think of the confusion a prospect will have when you give them your huge, full item catalog. Too much generic selling gives too many reasons not to buy. Make it easy to do business with you. Focus on a simple sale!

Don't Pick Green Fruit

Most post-show sales efforts treat each prospect the same, as though they are ready to buy. Know that there are a few "ripe apple" sales opportunities after each show, but many more are long-term prospects. When you try to close a prospect before they are ready (ripe), it is like frying a green tomato. It takes a lot of additives to make the meal (deal) seem palatable, and in the end, the long-term business relationship is damaged or destroyed without the foundation in place.

For your salespeople making efforts to meet quotas and close business immediately following a trade show, know that technology has changed how information is sent and received. Although technology has allowed for easier delivery of your marketing, *technology has also placed barriers to the acceptance of your messages.*

You must first get the attention of your prospect in a way that does not "turn them off." *To start, simply ask the prospect for their permission to market to them, and then deliver on your promise exactly as they requested.*

In his must-read book for trade show marketers titled *How to Persuade People Who Don't Want to be Persuaded*, Joel Bauer listed the results of a study by Thomas Davenport and John Beck. In the study, Davenport and Beck stated, *"a marketing message that both evoked emotion and was personalized was twice as likely to be attended to as the messages without those attributes."* The message of the study was that generic, impersonal, boring messages tend not to be read.

Providing they did not throw it away at the Expo hall, the attendee will have their literature and stacks of mailings from each booth visited. The reason your follow-up messages should evoke emotion and be personal is that your prospect is bombarded with phone calls from sales people they do not know, and companies they do not remember. At this point, the prospect is in a defensive mode because they are being "sold." To increase your likelihood of reaching your target audience and being heard:

CONSIDER INSTEAD:

- Asking the prospect how they would like you to stay in touch, then plan an approach that mixes timely and informative emails, faxes, handwritten cards, and small, interest-specific mailings before the first phone call is made. Add value for the prospect.

- Asking the prospect when and how they would like to be followed up with, and do it! Make the up-front contract before you make the call. Make your booth habits focus on learning the needs of the prospect.

- Using a great tip by Joel Bauer in *How to Persuade People who Don't Want to Be Persuaded* and figure out a way to let your prospects sample your suggestion, idea, or service. According to Bauer, without a way to sample you, the prospect could doubt you and not act on your wishes.

A Ripe Customer

When your customer is ripe to give you an OPPORTUNITY for a sale, they will let you know after one of your systematic marketing touches. After all, when you have communicated with the prospect for weeks, months, and maybe years after the show, in the style they feel most comfortable with, then you should be the first call they make to start the sales process.

Remember, the prospect is warmed and informed by your speaking and relating to them in their natural Platinum style. So naturally, they will want to keep business going with the person who they feel a personal relationship with. And as a practitioner of The Platinum Rule, that will be you.

But don't misunderstand the relationship. Your goal of getting a sale should really start with getting the opportunity. In most cases, the company given the first opportunity to fulfill the needs of the project will ultimately get the sale. A sale does not happen without an opportunity to make the proposal. So move first for the opportunity.

Then, when you are given the opportunity, make sure that your salespeople build their case on the wants, needs, desires, and even the fears of the behavior styles of the persons involved. Don't stop the Platinum approach with your marketing; make sure the sales part of your process is also a practitioner of The Platinum Rule.

Make sure you get to harvest the results of all of your seed planting and cultivating. Using The Platinum Rule tenets in your sales approach will allow you as the farmer to reap the harvest you sowed.

BOX OFFICE REVENUES:

Measure and Report Your Show Results

If you ask most companies about measuring their results from shows and events, you will most likely hear either a flat "no," or talk about not being able to track or measure their results.

You can't measure results when you don't have a system in place to move the leads from prospect to customer! If you habitually hand your leads over to your Sales Reps to never hear from them again, you will certainly not be able to measure the results beyond a zero return!

We did an informal survey at the 2006 Fabtech fabricating machinery show in Atlanta, Georgia, and found that of 34 exhibitors surveyed at their booths, only two had a system in place to measure the results of their show, and of the two, none took their measurement beyond a 12-month timeframe. Interesting because the buying cycle of both companies doing the measuring was 14-18 months. They did not give themselves a chance to measure a "hit" from the show because they stopped too soon!

Especially when you are working with highly engineered or capital-intensive goods, you need to make sure you have a measurement and reporting system that runs at least as long as the typical buying cycle beyond the show. If the potential is high enough, and the prospect or customer is truly qualified, the measurement system should never end. Keep both your marketing and measuring locked in the "buy first or die first" program, unless the prospect requests that you discontinue your efforts.

Yardstick, Tape Measure, or Checking Account

The time criteria are very important in measuring your returns. Is the timeframe you measure results in short (yardstick), medium (tape measure), or long-term (checking account)?

To decide the best or most likely means of measurement for your products and services, you must first determine the typical buying cycle from prospect to customer. If you have a product or service that typically takes 14 months from prospect to sale, and you expect to measure your results from a show six months after the show ends, well, your numbers will most likely be low.

However, if you know the length of time it takes on the buying cycle, then tie both your measurement and expectations at or after the buying cycle term, and you will then achieve a more accurate description, regardless of the length of time it takes.

Return on Investment or Return on Objectives

ROI or ROO. That is the question!

Does your company seek a monetary return on their show investment, or do they look for a return on an objective for attending the show?

In our opinion, if you want, you can and should have both. It is indeed possible and desirable to show a return on the investment with a return on the objective.

Generally, return on investments are the long-term means to measure post-show sales directly tied to the efforts of the show, and return on objectives are the short-term means to measure the effectiveness of a new demo, product launch, prospect counts, etc.

If you know the difference between ROI and ROO, you can and should use them in tandem within your overall plan for each and every show you exhibit.

RIDE YOUR CYCLE:

Selling Cycle and Buying Cycle

There is a difference between the selling cycle and the buying cycle in most companies. The difference is the time expected for a salesperson to "sell" a project, and the time it will naturally take a typical prospect to "buy" a project. Usually the selling cycle is significantly shorter than the buying cycle of the prospect.

You cannot force prospects to buy your products and services, at least more than once. Promotions and incredible discounts merely borrow sales from future sources. Some people will buy today if the offer is attractive and compelling enough; however, one only need to look at the zero percent financing of the Big Three auto companies in 2005 to see that they borrowed future sales for a short-term boost. Then, once the time came when the future sales would have naturally happened, there was a void of activity, and the panic set in. Zero percent financing programs were again rolled out, and the borrowing from future sales was made to satisfy short-term profit expectations.

Make sure that your selling cycles and buying cycles are as synchronized as you can make them. When they move together, prospects are nurtured at the pace and manner dictated by their style and expressed interests. Now of course, Directors and Socializers will need to be moved at a faster pace and manner than the Thinkers and Relaters, but know the style of the prospect will allow you to speed up or slow down the delivery and content of your lead development, and therefore give the people what they really want.

Measure Results on the Calendar, not the Stopwatch

The ability to determine effectiveness and measure results will aid in developing future follow-up programs, show offerings, show results, and Sales Rep effectiveness.

- How do you measure the results from a trade show? Lead count, sales in a year, infinite sales, or profitability?

Companies looking to measure their results from a trade show need to first determine their goals and objectives for the show. Implement strategies and tactics to support the objectives.

Steve Miller again contributes to this book by quoting that "90% of exhibitors [he] interviewed have no measurable objectives for a trade show. If you don't measure, how do you know if you succeeded?"

Implement a formal lead conversion system that markets and tracks each lead, with an area to document any and all purchases from the prospect. Measure your results related to the goals, objectives, strategies, and tactics.

Miller recommends that you "extend" your trade show an extra day to begin the implantation of the leads into your marketing system, and start the follow-up and tracking programs while you are still at the show. Get the information down on each prospect and customer while everyone has fresh memories of their experience, and the notes that they took on the lead card. You want to make sure that all the information is accurate and makes sense before you go after your next series of touches with the attendees following the show.

Shout Your Successes

No one will be aware of the success of your show program if you don't report the results. After all, bad news travels fast, and good news is quickly in the past. In order to get additional buy-in to build your show program, you need to report or share your results with everyone in your company. Let those in charge of your trade show budgets see the results of your efforts. Leverage your triumphs as proof that your follow-up program works, and gain future budgets to support your efforts.

You are the only one who can be your own promoter or public relations expert. Just as important to the success of your program and the continued funding of your projects is to communicate the facts of your results.

Don't believe that you are bragging about your successes, because any news can be delivered in a way that is both humble, and will speak clearly to the overall behavioral types you need on your team. Especially if your have Directors and Thinkers to report to, make sure that your successes come in the form of data and profitability. Give them the facts and figures that they want, and you have a bulletproof way to guard your trade show budgets from cuts.

Expose Your Failures

A key to establishing and maintaining your credibility is to expose your failures when they arise. As important as it is to shout your success, exposing your failures adds believability to your show program. When people realize that you are willing to share all news, not just what makes you look good, they tend to believe you in good times and bad as you are perceived to have nothing to hide.

For many people, exposing their failures is tough, especially for the Thinker and Relater who spend their lives trying to plan in order to minimize failure. Directors and Socializers don't really care, and tend to quickly forget their failures. But regardless of your style, you need to have the reporting of results both good and bad as part of your plan.

When you expose your failures, you should also consider asking for help from anyone you believe can help you, especially your superiors. People are inclined to want to help someone else, and have a sense of pride when they are asked to share their expertise to solve a problem. You don't have to do it alone (remember this Thinkers and Directors), so humble yourself enough to get outside help. When you work your plan in the manner that exposes everything, you get credibility that you will need to carry you through the difficult times.

Adjust Your Plan

Part of any great trade show plan is the ability and willingness to adjust the plan. Every show plan has areas that can use improvement, both minor and major, and the consideration of adjustments should be part of your review process.

In rare cases you will need a total overhaul of your plan. When this happens, make sure you use Platinum Rules to develop the heart of the new plan. But in most cases, you will need to make the fine adjustments, mostly based on exit interview feedback and staff interviews.

You can also have different plans for different industries. If you have an industry where you "own" the marketplace, your plan will reflect the position of industry leader. When you are in another industry or market where you are working toward market penetration and exposure, you will adjust your basic plan to accomplish these changes. In most cases, the adjustment will be reflected in the types of messages you will put forth.

Be active in your efforts to adjust your plan, and you will find that as each year goes by, your show program takes a proactive rather than reactive approach, i.e., you stay ahead of the curve and by this approach, ahead of your competition.

Lather, Rinse, Repeat

The saying "lather, rinse, repeat" is something most of us know from reading the labels on shampoo bottles. It indicates the need to have a repeatable, systematic approach to the process of washing your hair. However, the premise is also valid in the trade show industry. Most companies go from show to show without a definite plan to execute from an "A to Z" perspective.

The reason to go with the "lather, rinse, repeat" scenario is to operate in a manner that will allow you to track and measure the results of your actions. When you do not have consistency in your actions, it is difficult to establish the means to measure on a show-to-show basis.

We understand that every show is different, and you certainly need the Plan B in place for each circumstance. But do your best to keep the basic elements of your show plan in place, and repeat them for each show you do. Make adjustments when necessary, and continue to monitor your results. But have that system in place, and execute your plan each and every show. Make sure that each member of your team knows their roles and responsibilities, and is held accountable for doing their part.

The bonus is that the systematic, accountable approach to working a show will certainly make the Relaters and Thinkers happy, and will give the Socializers and Directors at least a framework to consider should they get bored with doing it their own way!

SECTION IV

Winning with Platinum Rules Beyond the Exhibit Hall

W e developed this section of the book to give you more powerful strategies, techniques, and applications to apply the effectiveness of The Platinum Rule to your work and life beyond the trade show itself. We especially give you advanced strategies to use Platinum Rules in corporate events, the ultimate leverage in Platinum Rule application.

Use these techniques to build and maintain high-quality relationships of mutual benefit in your personal and professional life. Take The Platinum Rule into your office, as well as your family and home. Then, when other people see you as "someone different" and "more believable" on a regular basis, you will have gained the ultimate personal positioning; a Trusted Advisor.

OFF BROADWAY:
Conduct Platinum Events with Your Trade Shows

The hottest trend in the exhibiting marketplace is producing an event in conjunction with your trade show. Why are corporate events the hottest trend? According to Event Consulting Expert Diane Silberstein of Global Connections in Atlanta, Georgia, a properly planned and executed event is mostly about LEVERAGE. We give tremendous credit to Diane for her contributions to the event section of this book. Her guidance was the leverage we needed to bring you The Platinum Rules beyond the exhibit hall.

The Platinum Rule is about leveraging your own behavioral style with style of the other person. A corporate event held in conjunction with your show expands and leverages the opportunity to interact with your audience. Leverage the tradeshow by orchestrating time with your best clients, prospects, and key employees.

With a corporate event, you can expand your presence and image beyond the show floor while offering an EXPERIENCE to your target audience. The event is a natural extension of what you are doing in and around your booth, so continue the booth experience to wherever the event is held. A successful event should fit like a glove with your overall theme and marketing message of the show experience.

EVENTS AT SHOWS:
No Party, no Disco, no Foolin' Around

When you expand your presence beyond the show floor, your prospects and customers experience what it's like to be a member of your corporate family. Especially since they contribute to the well being of everyone involved in the "family."

A great event has a purpose, a game plan, and a measurable outcome as the foundation of the experience. Therefore, produce your event as an experience, remembered as more than a "party." The fact that corporate resources—human and monetary—are spent to produce the event underscores the importance of training and promoting the purpose, plan, and outcome with every member of your team.

Although a game plan is critical to take an event beyond the "party" classification, you always need to promote the event both internally with your people and externally with your audience. The promoted event is especially important if it is an open event to the public at the show. To promote your event among the show, leak out enough information through the media center to create a "buzz" on the show floor related to your event. Invite members of the media to your event to leverage your company, your people, and your brand.

Other attendees and exhibitors will likely hear about your well-planned, exclusive event and will look for a way to get in on the action. If attendees and competitors are talking about your event, it will have more power with your target audience. Also remember, the more unique the location, the greater the "buzz" on the show floor.

Goals are also important in building the foundation of your event planning. Different events might have different goals. Whatever goals you choose to meet, choose them well in advance of the event. Train your people with the strategies and tactics to meet your event goals. Understand that event goals can also be intermediate steps to a bottom-line goal. As an example of intermediate goals, we present five for your consideration:

Intermediate Goal 1: Create an experience with your company that is not about products and services, but about your people and your company

Intermediate Goal 2: Encourage interactions between people of compatible behavioral styles by creating opportunities for them to meet and interact

Intermediate Goal 3: Develop deeper, stronger relationships with your current customers

Intermediate Goal 4: Jump-start the trust and credibility process with your platinum list of prospects

Intermediate Goal 5: Lay the groundwork for future discussions of your products or services

So to summarize, the key to successful events is to keep them from being just a corporate party. Have a purpose, a plan, and a measurable outcome. Use the event to leverage the opportunity of having your people in one place at one time. Take the time with your prospects to inform, educate, and entertain. Use the event and your people to build goodwill with your prospects and customers, leveraging your investment of time and money for at least the next year beyond the show.

Making the Platinum Guest List

The Platinum Guest List—a vital starting point for any event.

As a practitioner of The Platinum Rule, you should already understand the communications preferences of your loyal customers. Be sure to include this information in your customer database for easy reference. The behavioral styles of your key prospects may be more difficult to determine, so consider their most-likely behavioral styles in your communications. Use the key words and phrases in the tables from the "Compelling Booth Presentations" and "Listening to Your Space Invaders" sections of this book. Use Platinum Rule behavioral style knowledge to start building trust and credibility as you build new relationships.

With any good business, relationships are your keys to success. Leverage customer relationships from more than just the sales level! It is very important to remember management and the technical folks as well. Make a multi-pronged approach with your key people. Participation from all levels of your company is key to the interaction with your prospects. Make your event an interactive experience if possible because interactive events are the most memorable and successful.

In order to make the event interactive, you have to deploy your event team to strategically "work" the room. How should you deploy your event team to work the room? By having a blend of the four behavioral styles: i.e. Directors, Socializers, Relaters, and Thinkers. Match your event team by assigning them to key prospects and customers that have similar styles. Leverage the comfort of similar behavioral style interactions to move the relationship to the next level.

Bait the Hook

What are the best ways to generate interest in the event? Event interest should start with the invitation. Since first impressions are very lasting, consider the invitation as "personal marketing" between your sender and the prospect. The invitation doesn't have to be the traditional engraved style, but it should be both personal and professional. Avoid a mass-produced message; instead, make sure the invitation contains some handwritten lines.

Quick and cheap means of communications will be viewed that way by your prospects and customers--cheap and with low importance. If you are going to invest the time, money and effort to produce an event, let your invitation reflect that. The invitation is your initial opportunity for a great first impression with your target audience, so make sure you bait the hook with the right bait.

How you communicate the message is also important. Consider having the message sent from a person on your team, not from "the company." The higher level in the company the sender resides, the better.

Let the guest know another human being of importance is personally inviting them. They are more likely to respond.

Communicate information in their preferred style. Technology has provided an entirely new invitation medium — the E-vite. When creatively and professionally developed, E-vites are perfectly acceptable for most corporate events. For your highest value prospects and customers, make sure that the invitation is handwritten on a hardcopy invitation.

Regardless of the invitation form, 10 key items should be included:

1.   The corporate logo, if appropriate

2.   Name of the host

3.   Invitation phrase such as "cordially invites you"

4.   Event type: reception, dinner, etc.

5.   Purpose of the event: "to celebrate", 'to launch", "to announce"

6.   Date

7.   Time

8.   Location

9.   Special instructions such as dress

10.   Where to reply

If an event is worth attending, it is worth requesting an RSVP. Use this opportunity to capture additional information about your guests such as contact info verification, dietary considerations, or anything else you need to know. Provide your audience the ability to communicate their attendance status to you via phone, fax or web response. This is a great way of providing guests multiple opportunities to address their special needs and expectations.

Your "A" Team

When you put together your event team, don't make the mistake of assigning only the Socializers. Strive for a balance in the team to accomplish the goals for the event and match your guest list. However, if your customer base tends towards one or two styles, then stock your team heavily with those styles.

Directors are the action/negotiators for your team. They typically work with the vendors and the results-oriented customers and prospects.

Socializers are great at "working the room." Even if you have a large percentage of guests that are not Socializers, it is good to have them on the team to keep the mood light. Not necessarily to entertain, but to have guests feel warm and welcome and make the event livelier and less stagnant.

Relaters offer calm in the chaos. Should anything happen during the event that is stressful, the Relater will be the glue to hold everything together and will keep lines of communications flowing. Relaters consider people's feelings and want everyone to feel they belong. Directors and Thinkers tend not to do this. Relaters are also very good listeners, and like to empathize with other points of view.

Thinkers are important because they are concerned with budgets, schedules, and details. You want the event to be on time and on budget? You want the i's dotted and the t's crossed? Planning and executing an event requires a lot of attention to detail. Thinkers are great at these jobs. During the course of the event, Thinkers are many times the best technical people and are great resources on the spot.

Superdome or Secret Hideaway?

When you think about the event venue, there are numerous options and considerations. The following list contains the main areas on which to focus the efforts of your pre-event plans.

Venue Size: Are you conducting a large-scale event designed to reach the masses, or do you want an exclusive intimate event where people will interact more closely?

Location: Is the event within the expo hall itself, at an adjoining hotel within walking distance, or completely off-site where you require transportation?

Unique: Is the venue truly important to your event for impression, "buzz" or theme? Is it possible to transform the ballroom at the expo hall or hotel into the "experience" you want? Consider the most likely Platinum Rule behavior styles to match the theme and create the right experience.

Budget: All of the items above will affect this important line item. Your choice of venue will also affect transportation and decorating costs. Do not consider the budget lightly, and always have a percentage cushion to move either way. If you have unexpected expenses, plan in advance to have funds to cover them.

Make sure to consider budget, uniqueness, and venue size in addition to the location. When you account for the size of your audience, their needs on a personal level and of course the budget, you increase the likelihood of creating a winning event for yourself and your audience.

Roll Out the Platinum Carpet

When you plan the look and feel of your event, you need to set the stage by rolling out the platinum carpet for your guests. Consider the timing or 'show flow' by creating schedule, the "look" or decor, and the layout of the functional and social spaces.

Social areas are where the real action takes place. To appeal to everyone, consider areas where the four styles will migrate and congregate. Keep in mind these tips:

- Thinkers are comfortable with technical areas, displays, venue details like historical buildings, museums, exhibits.

- Socializers prefer beverage stations, food displays and entertainment.

- Directors migrate away from the noise into more private areas where they can "get things done" and not be bothered by the Socializers.

- Relaters don't need their own space but will move in and out of the common areas. They will try to stay out of the way of the Directors, will peek in on the Thinkers, and move in and out of the Socializers.

When your guest list is firm, make it easy for YOUR people to match with prospects and clients of similar styles. If you are flexible and integrate your event team so that the behavior and preferences of your guests are met, you keep the guests comfortable.

Food and beverage may not necessarily reflect a style, but it certainly plays a role with special dietary needs. Know in advance if any of your guests have cultural, religious or medical needs for certain food or drink. If you let them know you considered their needs on a personal level, they will take note of your consideration. Nothing will keep a person longer at your event than when they are enjoying their surroundings: ambience, conversation, entertainment and food. First impressions are lasting, and as Malcom Gladwell correctly put in his book _Blink_, they happen in the first five seconds of meeting someone.

Décor sets the stage from the moment your guests arrive. Use lighting, color, props to create the theme, define the various areas of your event and move people where you want them to be. What is the overall image you wish to leave with your guests?

Entertainment should reflect what speaks to the various styles of the attendees as well as enhance the ambience. Make your guests comfortable by choosing entertainment to match their age, gender and whether they are stag or drag. Consider a variety of entertainment styles throughout the event.

Be conscious of your pace with Thinkers, the noise level with Directors, and the rate of guest inclusion with Relaters, and playful music and entertainment for Socializers. Be very, very considerate of your entertainment with the styles of your target audience. You can easily eliminate weeks and months of trust and credibility with improper or offensive entertainment.

Souvenirs from the event are also a nice touch to help remember you and your company. However, when you give souvenirs, they should be purposeful. Make sure the souvenir is something of significant or lasting value to the attendee. Based on behavioral styles, consider the following for your souvenirs:

- Memorabilia typically does not influence Directors.

- Thinkers like souvenirs if the item helps them be more precise and logical in its use. A small USB pocket flash drive is good for Thinkers.

- Relaters like items that make everyone look and feel good.

- Socializers like items that let them share a few laughs with others, or give a personal memory of the event like a drawing or photo.

Whatever the item, it should be in good taste and likely to be appreciated by the majority of your guests in attendance. Anything that the attendees can take home to their children is generally appreciated. Anyone with kids at home will tell you this!

The Post-Event Review

One of the biggest challenges you will face at a Platinum Rule event is to keep your people on-task and on-point. As discussed earlier, a corporate event is no "party." It's important to keep your event team focused on their role in the overall goals and outcomes of the event.

During the post-event analysis, you should determine if your goals, objectives, and strategies were really within your range of capabilities. If for example your goal is a 50% commitment rate for a post-event meeting and your room is full of Thinkers and Relaters, the goal might be unrealistic. However, if your room is mostly Socializers and Directors, a 50% rate might not be out of the question as these styles are fast moving and like to get to the end game as soon as possible.

The prevailing thought here is that, just like the trade show, you must take an honest look at post-event results to determine the effectiveness of your event program. Be prepared to repeat, modify, or replace your event program. Make sure the selection of your event analysis criteria, whatever you decide it is, occurs well before the event and not after.

Always keep in mind that your event team styles affect your analysis. Thinkers have a different set of criteria than Socializers and Directors certainly look for a different set of results than Relaters. Performing an analysis that considers the prospect and customer needs, aligned with the goals of your company will give you a common platform for your team review.

Encore! Encore!

The general excuse for top management to reduce an event budget is "we don't know if these events result in business." It is difficult to dispute the unsupported accusation of unknown results when you don't have a goal, as well as a means to measure the performance against the goal.

Successful event teams will develop, purchase, or consult an event planning and measurement system to track performance against their goals. You also need the will and the budget to track performance of your event goals. The importance of having a system or systems for event planning, execution, and measurement cannot be overemphasized. The reward is that with systems in place, you will have a way to produce the data to evaluate the success of your event program.

If your events fail to meet the established goals by your measurement, then top management has justification for their claims. But if you consistently meet and exceed the established goals and can show them the results in facts and figures, you will have the leverage to ask management for an increased budget to produce better, more productive events.

When you build and create an event program that works, and develop a team that knows their role and executes exactly each time, you will leverage your presence at trade shows. When you are successful in reaching event goals on a consistent basis, consider every trade show to include a concurrent event.

Leverage your event as an automatic extension of your show experience for your prospects and customers. Then, with systems in place to track and measure results, you can then accurately determine if an adjustment, replacement, or an encore is warranted.

PLATINUM RULES THAT PAY:
Capture More Post-Show Sales with Less Effort

The idea of accomplishing more with less effort appeals to everyone. However, when most people think about converting trade show leads into customers, they believe the level of effort is too high. In a traditional program of working a show lead into a customer, the level of time and effort required is high and tends to discourage follow-up beyond a few phone calls.

A better way to convert your leads into customers combines your knowledge of The Platinum Rule with relationship based, semi-automated lead development technology. Our choice of systems to develop our leads with less effort is the Cyrano System. (www.cyranogroup.com) The availability of this Platinum Rule based technology gives a "Lead Farmer" the opportunity to leverage their time to better serve their current customers while still cultivating the seeds of future business.

In this section, we show you the most important points to know when establishing your leveraged lead development program, and the best new ways to integrate Platinum Rules within lead development. Use these points within an intelligent, semi-automated lead system and dramatically increase your post-show sales.

Traditional Selling Roadblocks

In traditional selling, the salesperson asks "closed" questions frequently meant to force the prospect to say "yes," such as the forced-choice close, the sharp angle close, closing on the final objection, or the "I want to think it over" close. Here is where the salesperson really tries to take total control of the sales situation *and* the customer. This creates problems in the relationship that can damage or end the relationship prematurely.

Selling techniques with trade show leads is usually a bad idea. For most leads, they are not in a buying mode. From previous chapters, you learned that you couldn't force a person into a buying mode. Instead, you can help them learn as much about your value and thereby be the first choice when the buying mode happens.

As a defense mechanism to ward off the salesperson, many prospects will give you false or misleading answers to your probing questions.

This places you out of the realm of trusted helper and advisor and into the position as predator. The predator position does not create the trust and good will that will lead to future sales.

As a Platinum Rule practitioner of good trade show etiquette in listening and learning, you won't be forced to ask the closed-end questions to get the smokescreen or brush-off. You will instead LOVE to ask the open-ended questions because your interest is in the way they prospect answers the questions, not so much the answers themselves. You certainly learn more about the true wants and needs of someone when you ask good questions and then close your mouth and open your ears. Make sure you document what is said for pace, directness, and content.

If you insist on pressing a prospect into a corner, many times you get a smokescreen. Any smokescreen retards the relationship or obscures the decision-making process. If you hear "Your price is too high," and "I want to think about it," you have just heard a smokescreen. Both indicate that the prospect is uncomfortable with you and are communicating their uncertainty; they are avoiding telling you their true feelings and thoughts. What they are *not* telling you are their true concerns. But your behavior in the booth and beyond the show should not reflect this type of selling, unless of course they are a die-hard Director and WANT you to ask them these questions.

The Platinum Sales Cheat Sheet

Everyone wants is to sell more from their show leads. However, the skills to sell more from trade show leads starts at the moment of first contact and continues through the lifetime of the relationship.

To help you prepare for the beginning of the show, and to refresh your Platinum Rule skills during the show, we present a "cheat sheet" to selling to the four behavioral styles. Learn the following chart, make the strategies a part of your everyday dealings with your prospects and customers, and reap the rewards of greater leads-to-sales results.

Directors

- Be prepared, organized and fast-paced.

- Greet them in a professional manner.

- Learn and study their goals and objectives.

- Find out what they want to accomplish, how they are currently motivated to accomplish tasks and what they would like to change.

- Get to the key points quickly.

- Suggest solutions with clearly defined (and agreed upon) consequences... in addition to rewards that relate specifically to their goals.

- Provide two or three "best bet" options (in writing if possible) and let them make the decision on the best course of action.

- Make it obvious that you do not intend to waste their time.

Socializers

- Introduce yourself in a friendly, informal manner.

- Show that you are interested in them.

- Let them carry the conversation; let your enthusiasm for their ideas emerge.

- Be flexible in jumping to new topics that interest them.

- Support their hopes, dreams and ideas.

- Illustrate your ideas and benefits with stories and emotional descriptions that help them relate back to their goals and interests.

- Give them dramatic, emotion-laden testimonials.

- Clearly summarize details and direct them toward mutually agreeable objectives and action steps.

- Provide them with incentives to encourage quicker decisions.

Thinkers

- Be prepared, so that you can accurately answer their questions.

- Greet them cordially and proceed quickly to the tasks at hand; do not lead with small talk.

- Be willing to research answers to questions you cannot answer on the spot.

- Hone your skills in logic and practicality.

- Ask questions that demonstrate an understanding of their industry and reveal a clear direction of thought.

- Document both how and why a benefit or solution applies to their needs.

- Give them plenty of time to think; avoid pushing them into hasty decisions.

- Point out the pros and the cons of your products and services; offering the complete story will build credibility.

- Follow through on every promise... big or small.

Relaters

- Get to know them personally; greet them in a warm, friendly (but professional) manner.

- Develop trust, friendship and credibility at a relatively slow pace.

- Ask them to identify their own fears and emotional needs after clarifying the tasks and/or needs of their company.

- Demonstrate how your solutions will positively affect their relationships and help them better support their team.

- Avoid rushing them; provide personal but concrete reassurances as you move along.

- Be sure to cover, point-by-point, how what you're offering is a complete solution.

- Communicate with them consistently over long periods of time.

Learning these identification and adaptation skills will help you get your proverbial foot in the door. The next step is to build immediate rapport with the prospect. If you form a quick connection, you are well on your way to getting them to share their goals, dreams, desires and challenges. Remember, you want the person to move as quickly as possible to the "trusted friend" point in your relationship. There is no better way to do so than to make a positive, personal impression with a prospect in your booth.

Dealing with Customer Concerns the Platinum Way

Customer concerns are a given in today's economy. Every company claims that they are the fastest, cheapest, best, biggest, etc. Customers and prospects hear those claims hundreds of times each day. So much that they don't really believe. Concerns are sure to follow.

When a customer has a concern, you merely need to look to The Platinum Rule Cheat Sheet to see how each style prefers to communicate, and then go to them with either the facts and details (Relaters/Thinkers), or the bottom-line benefits (Directors/Socializers). A "concern" is usually an opportunity for you to reassure your prospect or customer that you indeed hear and understand them, and there is no better way to communicate your understanding than by using Platinum Rules.

We caution you in dealing with prospect and customer concerns to realize no one cares how much you know until they know how much you care. Customers don't always want to hear your expertise at first; they would rather know that you understand their point of view and share their concerns with them. That is why you make the effort to match their pace and give them the information their natural style dictates. Then you will be known as someone who cares.

After you are accepted as knowing the concerns of the other person, you may use your expertise to help solve the problem. Again, be direct when speaking with Directors and Socializers, and be less direct when speaking with Relaters and Thinkers. Be faster paced with the Director/Socializer people, and slower and more detailed with the Relater/Thinker people.

In the end, you will be able to move past prospect and customer concerns faster and more successfully when you use The Platinum Rules to let people know you hear them, understand them, and respect their needs for straight answers and/or details and facts.

Why you Love to Hear Your Name

Dale Carnegie said it in his classic best seller, _How to Win Friends and Influence People_, that "the sweetest sound in the world is your name." And he is right; people really respond when you use their names in your communications. Just make sure that you don't overdo it. Make the connection almost as though you were engaged in a verbal conversation. And if you know their style, make the connection using their name according to their style preference.

An example of name effectiveness is when you see junk email riddled with your name. You know that it was automatically generated; yet you still read it when it has your name. Almost like looking through a roll of photographs, you almost always look to see where your picture is first.

To dramatically increase your personal impact with others, strive to use their name in your written and verbal communications, even in your brochures if you have print-on-demand capability. Let the other person know you are speaking directly to THEM, and do not give them a chance to remotely think that you do not know who they are, and most importantly, their name.

A distant second in your direct and personal communications is to change the viewpoint in which you write marketing messages by using the word "you." When you change your marketing and messages from "customers will really love the time savings of our new widget" to "you will really love the time savings of our new widget," it places the effect of the message right to the reader on a personal level.

This appeals especially to Socializers. Then, when you have enough information to go to "Rachael, you will really love the time savings of our new widget," then you will hit a home run with your audience.

Remember how sweet it is to hear or read your name, and then turn that sweetness around and share it with your prospects and customers. They will reward you by remembering your name and calling you for an opportunity when it comes time for them to buy.

Marketing That Salespeople Love

For years, there has been a huge divide between the sales and marketing departments within most companies. Even though the company may have a V.P. of Sales and Marketing, the reality is that marketing has tended toward an advertising mentality, while sales feels abandoned or even betrayed by the ways marketing dollars are spent.

The change is made when you take your company to the level that aligns marketing in the role of directly supporting the sales function. Instead of marketing taking their dollars and spending them in hopes of building a "brand" or "awareness" to the masses, they use the money to support the branding and awareness of your people and products to one person at a time. And that "personal marketing" is the type of marketing sales people love.

When you take your marketing dollars and resources and allocate them in a personalized, targeted fashion, you help the salesperson convert them into long-term customers. And when you use Platinum Rules to personally market to the prospect or customer, speaking to them in their natural behavioral style, using the pace most comfortable to them, you stand the best chance of converting a substantially larger percentage, and keeping them as long-term clients.

With Platinum Rule marketing, you will see your average marketing cost per prospect go up tremendously. For example, you may see your marketing dollars go from .50 per prospect to $50 per prospect, especially when you have to develop the lead for a year or more. But look after that year to the amount of revenue you reap from the prospects that become customers. They may repay your $50 investment in them with an order for $5,000 or more. Not a bad rate of return!

The key to personal marketing mastery is that you do it at the prospect's natural pace and speak to them in the benefits statements that fit their style. The payoff is a dramatic increase in your lifetime returns from the marketing investment. When you take into account the preferences of the customer, treat prospects as individuals and not groups, and take a sniper's approach rather than a shotgun approach to the masses, your salespeople will see the benefits through increased sales and become your allies rather than adversaries.

Why CRM is a Four-Letter Word

Ask any person who uses a traditional CRM (customer relations management) system if they really believe it makes their job easier, and most likely you will get an unpleasant response about hitting the "snooze" button on a huge list of useless reminders or in some cases profanity! These reminders certainly do not make your list of tasks shorter, as promised by the software sellers, but instead have placed another pebble in your shoe!

The truth is that most CRM systems are long on promises to make your life as a prospect lead developer easier, and short on actually reducing your work load. In truth, CRM systems are masters at archiving your prospect and customer contact information and history, but do not have the ability to plan into the future for many of your activities.

The good part is that some progressive CRM systems are improving in their ability to be personal and pro-active in their use, with the best ones being web-based and accessible from any web computer. This allows you to work with your system from within the show hall, in your hotel room, or on the road. And many will now generate letters and mailings that are mail-merged with the name of the person. But behavioral style is generally overlooked. The ability to communicate with a prospect or customer using their natural style is where you need to be, and if possible, find a CRM system that will allow for sorting and messaging using style-based communications.

CRM alone is not the answer to post-show and post-event lead development. You need to know this before you are told or sold that CRM will be the solution to your lost lead opportunities. But intelligent CRM systems are out there, and in the next section, we will discuss one of these.

Someone to Do Your Work

When it comes to using a lead development system, you want to use a system that performs most of the work for you, rather than remind you of what you have to do. We use The Cyrano System (www.cyranogroup.com) to automatically send out follow-ups to our prospects and clients for months and years after the show ends.

As previously stated, CRM systems are improperly used and widely scorned as a contact information archive. They are great at reminding you of what you need to do, and when you need to do it, but fall short of actually doing anything to lessen your burden of work each day.

That is why systems like the Cyrano System are revolutionary in their approach to lead development and customer management. Cyrano takes your input on what you would like a customer or prospect to receive (style related), when you want them to receive it by scheduling delivery into the future (pace related), and the types of messages and language they contain (a function of direct vs. indirect) and molds this all into a web-based system that will do most of your work for you. Almost like having a web-based personal assistant!

The way Cyrano does the work for you is by having your requests to send gifts, brochures, letters, cards, and other information sent directly to a fulfillment house which prints, packages, and mails each of these items for you on a daily or weekly basis. You no longer have to remember to send out a brochure or a birthday card or gift to a key client, you just schedule the item with Cyrano, and it is sent out automatically for you, from you, on the exact day.

Typically, you are billed a small licensing fee for these types of systems, and you of course pay for each item you pick, package, and mail to your prospects and clients. But the peace of mind of knowing that the job is done tirelessly each and every day is worth the price, not to mention that you get to market to your prospect and customer base in a personal way familiar to their style, and at the pace that best suits them, not you!

Outsource Your Leads?

A huge trend in today's trade show and events marketplace is to outsource your leads to a company that specializes in qualification and development of your leads, on behalf of you and your people. Forget launching your expensive and valuable leads into the black hole of your Sales Reps' desk, forever losing the control and destiny of the lead; instead send it to the pros that are equipped to do the job your salespeople are not built to do.

Smart companies who do more than six trade shows and events per year find that for a small fee, each and every lead you get is warmed, informed, and developed on behalf of you and your salespeople. This service is done for as long as you wish, usually around the typical buying cycle of your products and services. You can pick the number of touches you want to go out, and the expense of each and every touch.

When outsourcing your leads, choose a company that has a reputation for flawlessly and systematically delivering your marketing, especially if they use Platinum Rules. If we are asked to manage a lead development for a company, we also use the Cyrano System. We always know what has been sent, and what is scheduled to send. By just a mouse click, we can see the status of each and every lead, and be able to access the data and change the commands from any web-based interface. Therefore, we don't ever lose a lead to a non-existent system or the circular file of a Sales Rep.

If you want to know the status of each and every prospect and customer, consider outsourcing your leads or using a system like Cyrano. If you take a systems approach to doing the work for you, you never have to report to your boss that you "ask the Reps" where the leads went. That alone should make most any Sales or Marketing Manager sleep better at night!

CEMENT THE PARTNERSHIP:

Grow Your Prospect and Customer Relationship Past the First Sale

Top salespeople make sure they are positively clear about the customer's expectations... the criteria they use to judge the success of the purchase. If you have done The Platinum Rule evaluation properly, you should be thoroughly familiar with their criteria. Be sure to monitor the criteria and stay involved in the ongoing life of the customer. For many salespeople, this means a consistent follow-up schedule. While every product or servicing cycle is different, there are standard follow-ups that all top salespeople should incorporate into their sales process. Let's begin with the basic Platinum Rule approach.

First follow-up: "Thank you!" note

Follow-up starts with a handwritten "thank you" note immediately after the sale. It is amazing how many salespeople still overlook this simple step. Try it for a while and see how many of your customers mention it... or how many of your notes wind up on their bulletin boards or displayed somewhere in their office.

Second follow-up: Check-up

The next follow-up is just to make sure they received the product and that it is working. For instance, a computer salesperson might call five days after the sale to make sure that the system is performing the way the customer expected. This initial check-up call is especially important for recognizing early on any problems or dissatisfactions. If the computer buyer has not been able to get his favorite software to work on your computer, they may be blaming you, the computer, your company, and life in general for a problem you could have fixed in five minutes. This call gives you a chance to preempt this problem before the potential emotional build-up that might lead to an unnecessary eruption.

Third follow-up: Gift

What better excuse do you have to contact a customer than to give him a present? Enhance every sale by following up within two or three weeks with a gift that represents a token of your appreciation... a little something extra. This should be something the customer did not expect to get and, ideally, it should enhance their product (or your service). It does not have to cost a lot but it should have a meaningful perceived value to the recipient.

Important note: You may consider *not* sending or delivering any gifts to Directors or Thinkers. Remember that these people primarily focus on tasks, results and processes, not relationships. A well-intentioned gift may be perceived as "wasteful" or a "business bribe" and produce the exact opposite result from what you intended. Additionally, some companies have policies that restrict or prohibit their employees from receiving gifts. A general rule of thumb (but not an absolute one) is to observe your customer's work environment. If you see items in their office with the logos of other companies, it's probably a safe bet that they would accept one of similar value from you.

Fourth follow-up: Referrals

This follow-up lets the customer know you are here to provide service and that you still care about their satisfaction. By this time, the customer has received your note of thanks and present and at least one call to make sure they were happy with their purchase. They should feel well taken care of and, if they are still happy with the product, they will probably be delighted to give you referrals. However, be reasonable in your expectations of gaining referrals from Directors and Thinkers. Remember that guarded people keep their relationships and/or their database under lock and key. Socializers and Relaters will most always be your best referral sources.

Of course you want to expand on these follow-ups to match or exceed the length of your typical buying or selling cycle. Give the prospect or customer many good reasons to partner with you, and give the reasons consistently over time, and your prospect will consistently reward your efforts with business opportunities.

Keep the Square Peg From the Round Hole

Everyone in sales has had the good fortune to be matched with a customer who is described as a "good fit" for them. However, not always does the salesperson know the real reasons why the good fit happens.

Automotive salespeople know that they tend to sell one out of four prospects they meet. The reason is that they will have the best opportunity to sell people who have a similar buying style to their selling style. Your best auto salespeople are the ones who adapt to the prospects' style and help them buy, not sell them.

Our goal for this section is to have you examine your salespeople and match your customer styles to a similar styled salesperson. By matching a Thinker customer with a Thinker salesperson, or a Socializer with a Socializer, etc., you increase your chance for sales, repeat business, and keep the proverbial square peg (your salesperson) from the round hole (your customer).

The Director Salesperson

A Director salesperson has the natural tendency to launch quickly into a sales presentation. They get right to the point by telling your prospect the bottom-line benefit of using your product to provide a solution. Their natural tendency is to spend little time on chitchat or getting to know your prospects... unless it's required to get the sale! Directors move quickly, and if a prospect does not see the benefit of your proposal, they move on to the next prospect.

Directors have a fast, efficient manner and total focus on goals that make them more comfortable than most people with cold calling. They are able to tolerate negatives as a necessary part of the sales process. Directors tend to sell by painting a convincing picture of the benefits of their product or service.

Their best "fit" is with standard products or services where a match can be determined. Products or services requiring lengthy tailoring, customization and/or development (such as complex computer, communication or consultation systems) try their patience. Directors prefer sales processes where quick decisions can be made based on rational, concrete, reality-based data.

Director salespeople are very careful about time... especially their own! They tend to make specific time appointments and arrive punctually. They are clear about their desired results from customer contacts and quickly present the features and benefits offered by their product or service.

The Socializer Salesperson

The Socializer salesperson has a positive attitude, is enthusiastic, optimistic and has a natural orientation toward people. Socializers are excellent at making contact, networking and socializing. They tend to get bored easily. Their best sales situation is one that gives them an opportunity to meet and greet a lot of people, without a lengthy negotiation process. Examples of products are real estate, cars, office equipment and club membership sales.

Socializers are great at painting mental pictures for customers. They may use sentences beginning with, "Just imagine yourself..." or "You'll be the envy of your neighbors when..."

Socializers like best a chance to work interactively with others and opportunities to give personal feedback and discussion to get – or stay – on course. They are best used when avoiding long-term projects that drag out and really like opportunities to start projects while letting others handle the follow-through and detail work.

The Thinker Salesperson

The natural style of the Thinker salesperson is to provide the prospect with lots of precise facts and logical information. Because Thinkers are not relationship oriented, they perform best in sales situations involving technical, faster moving products, where buying decisions are based primarily on technical capabilities. Thinkers work well with professional buyers, as they tend to give them an organized, logical presentation, without spending time on small talk.

Thinkers take the time to understand the needs of the customer, as well as the process in which the product or service is expected to perform. Their proposals tend to emphasize the technical features and superiority of their product or service. Thinkers try to provide a "bullet-proof" solution for their customers and are often surprised and disappointed if the purchase decision is made on a basis that is not completely "rational."

Thinker salespeople are painstaking information gatherers, and they carefully piece together the needs of the customer and the requirements of the organization before presenting a solution. Their natural style is to depend on their ability to provide solutions rather than focusing on the interpersonal relationships. They prefer selling scenarios where they can analyze the situation, map out a solution, and then leave any training, installation or follow-up to someone else.

The Relater Salesperson

The natural style of the Relater salesperson is to build relationships and to progress slowly and steadily through the sales process. They are very concerned with maintaining the relationship and making sure that they have the best possible solution for their customer. They spend a lot of time getting to know the customer personally and seek to understand their personal preferences and dislikes. They also use their listening talents to get an in-depth picture of the customer's needs and wants.

The Relater's ideal sales position is one that requires strong customer relationships and a service orientation. Systems or services that require months (or years) of repeated, incremental work to respond to known needs (and involve the same decision makers) are perfect for the Relater. Relaters maintain relationships with high levels of service, personal involvement, and attention to details.

The Relater salesperson seldom pushes for a close... or seldom needs to. Through their painstaking needs identification process and emphasis on knowing and understanding their customers, getting the customer's commitment flows out as an almost evolutionary part of the sales process. They also enjoy sales or service work that requires a team approach.

There is one weakness of the Relater as a salesperson: while it is true that their greatest strength is reading others, it can get in the way when working toward confirming a sale. After the sale they ask themselves, "What happens if the customer does not like the house, car, jewelry, etc. they bought?" This issue is one that a Relater salesperson must deal with to become more successful.

Your Unfair Customer Advantage

This section considers the dominant style of your customers, especially your best customers. When you know the style, or the most likely style, of the people that buy your products and services, it is easier to serve them based on their style needs. You can even use the following information to create marketing that will attract the types of customers you want!

Use this section as a guideline to market, sell, and understand the needs and wants of your clients and prospects. Conducting your business and relationship on these foundational Platinum Rule tenets will help prospects and customers feel comfortable with you. The comfort comes because you are able to anticipate and exceed their expectations, all based on what you know from their style.

The Director Customer

What this customer wants to know is how your product or service will solve their problems most effectively, right now. The Director is not a natural listener, so details and lengthy explanations are likely to be lost on him. The salesperson is expected to provide immediately useful information and recommendations that will move the Director toward his goals.

Time is an important factor for the goal-oriented Director. They do not tolerate having salespeople waste their time and do not want to waste theirs. This includes time spent on "unimportant" chitchat. Directors are more comfortable as team leaders than as team players.

Because of this, they tend to make decisions themselves rather than getting others involved.

Director customers will often ask detailed questions more as a test of the salesperson's credibility than because they want to know the answers. If it is necessary to provide detailed information to a Director, it should be done in writing so the Director can review it later.

Director customers look for product solutions that will help them achieve their goals. They maintain control of the sales process and prefer salespeople who provide the information and data necessary to make a sound decision. They are competitive and respond well to products or services that are "the best."

Directors expect results *now* and are impatient with waiting. They expect salespeople to respond to impossible deadlines even if it means sacrificing personal time. They aren't especially interested in developing relationships with the salesperson, but it is important for them to believe that the salesperson can help them get their results.

Directors like to have choices. They like to have options and exercise their decision-making power. Each possibility should be a reasonable choice backed by evidence supporting its probability of success. This type of buyer has clear objectives to achieve and responds to those who can demonstrate that their product or service can efficiently achieve results.

The Socializer Customer

The Socializer customer will make purchasing decisions quickly if they become excited by an opportunity placed before them. They dislike being bogged down with a lot of details and data about the features of the product or service, but will listen intently to the benefits. In fact, with their fast, creative minds, they often see the benefits before you can point them out. When this happens, compliment them for their quick thinking and their "big picture" vision, but otherwise... don't speak! At that moment, you are the *second-best salesperson* in the conversation... they will sell themselves.

Socializers base many of their decisions on intuition or first impressions. They need to be liked and admired; it helps if salespeople understand what makes them look good... both personally and professionally. They look for fun and creativity in the buying/selling process and respond well to invitations to social gatherings: lunches, golf outings, celebrations, etc. They prefer to know salespeople personally, and they want the salesperson to know their likes and dislikes.

Socializers do not like bureaucracy and paperwork. They want the sales process to be simple and easy... they want to say "yes" and then have everything magically happen without their further involvement. They are so positive and optimistic that they often expect more than the salesperson intended to deliver.

Socializers will go with a risky decision or a new product if they are convinced that it will help move them closer to their dream. It is also important for them to know there is not a steep learning curve to using a product or service. If they suspect so, they may decide against the purchase. As such, they expect the salesperson to be part of their "team" to help get them through the learning curve quickly.

The Thinker Customer

The Thinker customer is task-oriented and needs information and specific data to make his decision. Thinkers want to understand the process of the sale, as well as how the product or service will operate within their current systems. They need time to evaluate the data. They tend to respond positively to graphs and charts that visually clarify the information. All information presented to Thinkers should be well organized and logical.

Thinkers sometimes become lost in non-essential details (that they believe may have some hidden, less obvious significance). Helping them re-focus on the "big picture" and comparative benefits between competing choices can help them to accelerate their decisions.

Thinker customers respond well to efforts to reduce the buying risk. Guarantees, free trials and pilot programs can reduce obstacles to the Thinker's purchasing options. Compared to the other styles, Thinkers also tend to be concerned about the impact of the purchase decision on the organization: how it fits into policies, procedures, and existing circumstances. Thinkers seldom make their decisions based only on relationships, but it is important that they respect and trust the salesperson and his organization to "make right" any problems encountered after the purchase.

Thinkers have subdued body language and verbal responses, making them hard to "read." If you stop to think about it (pardon the pun), the Thinker is the easiest style to identify because of their low-key, deliberate, measured and reserved behaviors. They are put off by a perceived excess of either directness or uninformed enthusiasm by salespeople and view too much intensity as distracting and unnecessary. The Thinker customer wants to know that the salesperson is knowledgeable in his field.

Thinkers prefer a minimum of interaction and would rather have a few short phone calls than an intensive series of meetings. Thinker customers tend to avoid personal involvement and are more comfortable with discreet or formal buying procedures.

The Relater Customer

The Relater customer needs to have a relationship based upon personal assurances and trust prior to making a buying decision. Relaters tend to assemble a buying committee of advisors to help them make the decision because they want everyone affected by the purchase to have a say in the decision. Relaters are seldom in a hurry to make decisions and will be turned off by pushy, aggressive behavior.

Relaters respond to friendly attention and efforts to make them feel like a part of the customer/vendor team. They need to be personally at ease with the salesperson. They also want to understand how the operations of the company behind the salesperson might affect them. They want the salesperson to listen and be sensitive to their needs and situational requirements. Once they have established a strong relationship, they are likely to remain loyal to the salesperson... even in the face of competition.

Relaters expect salespeople to be available to make presentations to other people within the organization who might have an interest in the purchasing decision. They want to make sure that the decision will be completely accepted by their organization before making a final commitment. They also want assurance that they can depend on the salesperson to honor all commitments.

Relaters have difficulty saying "no" and may make excuses or create delays in order to get out of a difficult sales situation. They expect the salesperson to be in tune with their needs and feelings. When they feel that the salesperson does not understand or sincerely care about their situation, they withdraw or change the subject. There is one exception to this tendency: Relaters will say "no" rather quickly when they get the sense that a salesperson is lying or trying to sell them something that may be harmful to their company, family or personal security. They highly value excellent service and follow-up.

Secondly, satisfied Relater customers are excellent sources of referrals. Customers talk. They talk about poor service and they talk about extraordinary service. When they get super service, they refer their friends and relatives to the salesperson who delivered on his promises.

Without repeat business and referrals, a salesperson must constantly prospect and cold-call new accounts. That is not the way most salespeople want to spend their lives... and it certainly is not the best way to be successful!

When you first meet, you have a chance to begin building a good customer relationship. However, it is only *after* the first sale, when you make sure your customer is satisfied (preferably delighted!), that you really cement the relationship.

Platinum Customer Expectations

Regardless of the product or service you supply, there are many sources of your solution available to prospects and customers. Even if your competitors do not have exactly what you offer, in the mind of the prospect and customer, you can be replaced.

If you have applied the lessons in this book and earned the right to do business with a customer, you are now under their expectations for the future of the relationship. It is easy to move sales forward when everything works as expected, but the true test comes when something fails or falls through the cracks. It happens in every customer/supplier relationship, so prepare now your action plans. Customers expect that you will be there to save them when these things happen, and you are measured by your response to problems, not your sales and marketing skills.

World-renowned direct marketing expert Dan Kennedy in his subscriber newsletter *No B.S. Marketing to the Mass Affluent* describes a situation where one of his long-time suppliers of travel services had a dismal experience with a vendor. In the situation, the vendor clearly failed the customer in their services, even going so far as to damage their personal items in the process. The problem as Dan described was not in the experience, or even the damage, but the business managers treating the customer in an uncaring, unrepentant manner.

When the travel coordinator heard of the lack of proper follow-up in the poor service and damage, his remark was "they are dead to me." An account worth $50,000 annually had been eliminated by disregard and laziness on the part of the vendors' business manager.

You want to be regarded as someone who can be a savior in times of trouble. This section will give you the tools to make the difference in your customer relationships if and when things do not go as planned.

DON'T MEET BUT EXCEED:
Maintaining The Customer/Prospect Relationship Past the Sale

Assuring customer satisfaction is a secret ingredient of extraordinary sales success. You will benefit two ways by assuring the purchase of each customer. First, this increases the likelihood of repeat business. Almost all products have a life cycle and will be replaced or upgraded. Customers have a tendency to return to the salesperson who previously matched them with a product that met their needs and then provided them with superior follow-up care matching their behavioral style.

In traditional sales training, salespeople learn techniques to help them overcome objections. Nothing is more frustrating than to work hard exploring a prospect's needs and collaborating on creative solutions to their problems only to have them speak a last minute objection.

The first thing a **Platinum Rule** salesperson does in gaining an advantage in their situation is to change their terminology. They drop the word "objections" and call them "customer concerns," especially when discussing sticky situations with the customer. Talking about "objections" makes it sound like the customer is being difficult. In reality, they are not being difficult; they are expressing their concerns about the solution you have proposed.

The best way to end the "objection" game is to avoid it in the first place. If you do enough information gathering at the beginning of your sales relationship, and collaborate with your prospect on a solution, there should little left to object to.

If your client has a valid concern that proves that your solution is not right for them, you both will be better off discovering this before or during the sale, rather than after the deed is done. We should actually welcome it when a customer expresses their concerns because they are giving us information to guide us.

Part of dealing with concerns is to move past the discouragement that comes with them and actually welcome the opportunity they provide you to better understand your client's needs. Rather than being rejections, these concerns are course corrections. Clients are often reluctant to express their real concerns up-front... sometimes they do not even realize what their concerns are. Therefore, when they do express their concern, it gives you a chance to make sure you have the right solution that matches their needs.

View customer concerns as an opportunity, not a roadblock. Here are four steps to help you effectively deal with customer concerns:

1. **Listen:** Hear the customer out. Listen carefully for clues to help you reveal their real concern. Sometimes salespeople blow sales just by trying to jump in too soon and overcome an objection. Remember to hear out the concern completely prior to responding.

2. **Clarify:** Ask questions to make sure you have a complete understanding of the concern *from the customer's point of view.* What do they mean when they say the price is too high, they need to think about it, or they need to talk to a friend?

3. **Respond:** Respond appropriately to the concern. Refer back to the decision criteria you established in the Explore stage and make sure that each point is still valid. Review the benefits of your product to see where each criterion applies and where your product may fall short.

4. **Confirm:** Make sure the customer understands your response and is satisfied with it. Did it really answer his concern? You want to make sure that this same concern does not come up again.

The way we respond to our customer's concerns depends on the **type** of customer concern and the selling stage. Each stage of the sales process has different types of typical concerns. In the beginning, most are simply "put-offs." The prospect is trying to avoid dealing with the salesperson. In the later stages, the concerns most salespeople meet relate to product, price, postponement and personal style.

It is extremely important to handle personal style conflicts immediately. Reading and adapting to the styles of each customer are the foundations upon which everything else builds. If the relationship collapses, so does everything it supports. This happens because trust was broken; your sales style may not have been appropriate for the prospect or the prospect may not feel that you have a sincere interest in his goals. Somehow, you have lost the confidence of your prospect.

The best way to deal with the problem of "lost confidence" is to avoid it in the first place. If you are sincerely trying to help your clients and not sell them, they will never lose confidence in you. You have to listen more than you talk, always monitor how well you are relating with the customer, and do what you say you are going to do when you say you are going to do it. When there are problems or glitches... fix them and "make things right." Keep on top of your clients' changing needs, so you can alter your plans and policies as needed.

Whatever the cause for the style mismatch, you need to use all your communication skills to get the relationship back on track. You should review the prospect's style and make every effort to treat them appropriately.

PLATINUM PARTNERS PAY YOU BACK:
Prospect Referrals Bring Your Best Business

Don't forget to ask for referrals, and *how* you ask will determine your success. On a regular basis (determined by the life cycle of your product), you should check with your customer to make sure they are happy and satisfied with the solution you have provided. This gives you a chance to identify problems and provides opportunities for follow-on sales and more referrals.

Immediately after the post-sale follow-up, we would recommend that you ask each customer questions similar to:

- "John, we often put articles or case studies in our newsletter, brochures and on our website. You seem to be very satisfied with our product/service. I was wondering if we might be able to contact you in the future for your testimonial about our company?"

- "John, as you may recall, you found me through a referral from one of your friends/coworkers/clients/vendors. Because of our excellent reputation for delivering on our promises, we are growing almost exclusively through referrals. Who do you know who _____?" Of course, you will describe your ideal prospect and prompt John's memory for referrals. We describe this process in detail in our upcoming book: "_The Platinum Rule for Personal Marketing Mastery_."

- "John, I have found that it is much easier for me to keep my clients rather than running around looking for new ones. I am willing to work hard to earn your repeat business. I was wondering if you could tell me how, and how often, you would like for me to stay in contact with you over the coming months and years?"

If the customer is unwilling to give you referrals, you may be falling short of their expectations. This is a clear signal to review the product and the buyer's success criteria to see if they align. If you find an area where the customer feels like they have not received what they expected, you should acknowledge the problem and try to fix it. You might have to discuss all their future expectations to make sure that you both understand the process. If you have not met some of their expectations, you should offer some type of "compensation."

If you are going to survive in today's highly competitive environment, you have to have an excellent product... and *even better service*. If you cannot meet the customer's expectations, you are not going to be in business very long.

Problems give you a chance to show how much you care about the customer. To handle them correctly, you must immediately acknowledge the problem and take responsibility for your part in the problem. You then must to do whatever is possible to resolve the problem. This could be a letter of apology, partial or full refund, or replacement of a defective product.

You are more likely to be successful if you have a sound strategy in mind for this recovery. You will probably have to make concessions in order to re-establish the customer relationship, but the rewards are worth the effort. There is more at stake than the profit on just this one sale; all future sales and all future referrals from this customer depend on your ability to reaffirm your commitment to quality and service.

ASK AND YOU SHALL RECEIVE:
Referrals the Platinum Way

Consider the following approach to your future plans to gain referral business:

At First Order

- Thank you card/business card from the salesperson

Week One After First Order

- Phone call by salesperson to see if order fulfilled correctly
- Call by salesman day after delivery to ensure completeness

Week Two After First Order

- Ask for written testimonial about the completeness of the transaction and goods

Second Order

- Order acknowledged by phone and email
- Order fulfilled on a personal level
- Call by salesman day after delivery to ensure completeness
- Phone call 10 days later to ensure complete satisfaction and address any concerns

Third Order

- Order acknowledged by phone and email
- Order fulfilled on a personal level
- Call by salesman day after delivery to ensure completeness
- "Memory Jogger" letter or email to customer, asking them to think of any other people they know who could use your products or services
- Follow-up Memory Jogger two weeks after mailing with a phone call or letter
- Ask for referrals based on Memory Jogger answers

Fourth Order

- Order acknowledged by phone and email
- Order fulfilled on a personal level
- Ensure completeness by email or phone

Fifth Order

- Order acknowledged by phone and email
- Order fulfilled on a personal level
- Ensure completeness by email or phone

- Handwritten note to thank customer for business and relationship
- Ask for testimonial about recent transactions and great customer service

After one year

- Conduct meeting with customer to review relationship
- Review year in specific details
- Ask for referrals of likely and similar prospects

When you take the pro-active rather than reactive approach in dealing with your customers, assuring them of your commitment to their needs with each order, they will be most happy to help you with referral business.

Even if they cannot refer you personally, take note of their style, and ask them if you may use their testimony or even use a phone call to match them with another prospect who has a similar Platinum Rule style. Put the Thinkers with the Thinkers, and the Directors with the Directors, and then get out of the way! Let your investment of time and interest with your customer pay dividends in their attempt to pay you back by bringing another client into your "family."

By treating your customers in a Platinum Manner after each and every order, you can rely on them to sell you and your company to others who share their similar behavioral style.

DON'T BE AN ORPHAN IN YOUR CORPORATE FAMILY:
Live The Platinum Rule Each Day

Many professionals in the exhibit industry feel neglected in their corporate family. Few co-workers listen, understand, respect, or cooperate with them in their capacity as Exhibits and Events Manager. The feeling has been described to us as "feeling like an orphan."

A lack of support and understanding from the home office leads to trade show and events professionals feeling frustrated and unfulfilled in their challenge to bring prospects and profits back to the company.

Most exhibit professionals spend much of their time out of the office, living from show to show, not establishing personal and political bonds within the company. As a result, their efforts to gain cooperation and respect are sometimes met with resistance or apathy.

A lack of understanding on the part of the manager, and the distance of the relationship from the office because of travel, contributes to the isolation of the exhibit professional. To help the situation, you should analyze yourself, your role, and others, and discover what distinguishes you within your company.

Losing the "orphan" feeling starts with how you use your personal traits and your patterns of behavior in situations. Each person has their own traits, some positive and some negative, and how you use those traits makes the difference in the quality of your business and life.

Some of your personal traits could be: **caring, self-control, intelligence, vision, determination, carelessness, awareness, humility, acceptance,** and **self-correction.**

Your personal traits evolved into patterns of behavior over years. Your behavior patterns affect your success or failure in your relationships, and therefore affect the success or failure in your job. You can see in others the effects of their relationships as dictated by their behavior patterns. It does not matter how smart you are if you cannot get along with others.

If you are not getting the results you want, then correct your situation by a shift in your thinking, followed by a change in your behavior patterns. You cannot change your behavior until you change the way you think about someone, something, and especially yourself.

Taking the steps to change your thoughts is the first step to correcting your situation.

Changing behavior patterns that are years and even decades old takes time. However, changing the way you think can be done in a matter of minutes, purely by faith and choice. If you really want to engage the ideas we present and increase your personal influence with people, then follow this simple model:

1. Identify your personal traits

2. Write them down as either positive or negative to your situation

3. Change your thoughts, knowing that within your positive and negative traits lie the seeds for great opportunities

4. Choose one negative trait to eliminate and one positive trait to gain or improve

5. Watch your corresponding behavior patterns change with your actions

When you feel you've made real progress in lessening or eliminating a negative trait, choose another negative trait to eliminate. Then find a positive trait to replace the old negative trait and build upon your improved behavior pattern. It is like eating an elephant; you can do it by taking the task one bite at a time! Don't go for everything at once.

Grow your comfort with your personal development by asking a trusted friend to help you monitor changes in your behavior. Tell him or her that you're working on changing a behavior characteristic and you'd like their help in holding you accountable. Know that you will occasionally slip back into your old behavior patterns, but don't be too hard on yourself. After all, you've had more practice at the old pattern than the new positive trait you've embraced. Remind yourself that you're on the road to change even when you fall back into your old habits. It is like human nature to sometimes regress, but you will eventually find the new behavior patterns based on your positive traits as second nature.

Enjoy True Authority in Your Position

True authority refers to how well you know your particular area of expertise, your company, and your industry. Are you current regarding your company's strengths and weaknesses relative to competition? Are you familiar with the skills and techniques of being a good manager within your company? Do other people come to you with questions about your company and your industry because they respect your expertise? Or do your employees, peers, and superiors turn to others when they need answers? Does the depth of your knowledge project credibility and command respect from your employees and fellow workers? Or do you hear them say: "I could do her job as well as she can!"

The depth of your knowledge in the areas listed above has a profound effect on the true authority you have in your position. To improve true authority, make every effort to learn as much as possible about your company and your industry. Be thoroughly familiar with your firm's exhibit and overall policies and procedures. Get to know your products and people on a personal level. Study current situations and trends within your industry, and find out how your company rates within the industry compared to your competitors. Take advantage of any training programs your company may offer. By increasing the depth of your overall and specific area knowledge, you command respect from your employees, fellow workers, and superiors by projecting an image of intelligence and credibility.

The Importance of Global Knowledge

This area deals with your ability to converse with others in fields outside your area of expertise. What are the latest developments in world events? Are you familiar with the latest popular books and movies? Can you converse with people about things that are of interest to them, not just to you?

The responsibility for increasing the range of your knowledge falls to you and no one else. Regardless of your age or background, many options exist for increasing your global knowledge. We recommend that you read some form of information every day, from national and local newspapers to informational websites. Also, read a major news magazine each week to give you a good background in national and international events, as well as some additional knowledge in education, the arts, sports, books, movies, etc. Make an effort to read at least four books a year outside your normal area of interest, and try to mix in some spiritual, classic fiction and educational nonfiction.

By increasing the range of your knowledge, you will be able to develop easier rapport with others. Not restricting the topic of conversation to something you alone find interesting allows people to be more comfortable in speaking with you. Some will go out of their way to talk with you as they feel that you share something in common. Research has shown that the more people feel they have in common the better they like and trust each other. By increasing the range of your knowledge, you can increase your circle of influence with all types of people.

How To Increase Your Global Knowledge

To leverage your opportunities for learning, make better use of nonproductive time. Situations of non-productive time to target are driving to and from work, cooking, cleaning, waiting in line, and time normally spent surfing the Internet. You can make use of this nonproductive time by watching a television news show, going to a news web site, listening to radio news or talk shows, listening to books and/or educational materials on audio.

If you are not knowledgeable about another colleague or manager's favorite topic of conversation, show interest in it by doing your own research, asking questions, and letting them teach you! This is an effective and productive way to learn because other people love to teach, especially an area that is of great interest to them. Remember that increasing the range of your knowledge comes easily when you listen and interact with other people.

Time is Powerful

Time is used to show how we feel about the relative status and power of other people. When the president of the company calls a junior manager to their office for a meeting, the manager will probably arrive before the appointed time. Because of the difference in status, most managers would probably feel that any inconvenience in waiting should be on their time, not the president's. The president's time is regarded as worth more and therefore is not to be wasted. How do you use or abuse the time you are given in your workday?

Time is also used to define power and control within relationships. If two managers of equal status are very competitive, one might try to structure the other's time to demonstrate greater status and power.

For example: one manager calls the other and asks her to come to her office for a meeting. First, the initiation indicates a higher status. Second, specifying the place and time diminishes the other's influence. Third, the immediacy of the intended meeting implies that the other has nothing more important to do. If she agrees, the chances are high that the invited manager will not arrive for the meeting exactly at the agreed upon time. She will probably be a bit late and offer no apology. This is enough to irritate her colleague but not enough to represent an open insult. The silent message is: "My time is equal to yours, and I'm at least equal to you." Do you use time as a means to define power and control in your position? If so, does your use of time help or hurt your relationship with your colleagues?

Using time to manipulate or control others is common, although we are not usually aware of it. When we allow others to structure our time, we usually acknowledge their greater status or power. This is especially true when we allow a manipulation of our time when we would rather be doing something else. When you manipulate or allow for manipulation of your private time you exercise the use of time for power and control. We all know that private time is becoming more and more valued, as evidenced in the growing reluctance to work overtime in the evening or on weekends.

Waiting is another matter of the power of time. The longer we are kept waiting, the worse we feel. The longer we keep other people waiting, the worse they are likely to feel. Remember these points when you are looking to eliminate or grow one of your personal traits as listed earlier. You gain a greater respect and authority in your position when you respect the value of the time of others.

To illustrate the abuse of time for power and control, consider the situation of the middle manager summoned to a meeting with the president at 1:00 p.m. The middle manager arrives at a "respectful" 12:50. She remains comfortable until 1:10, when she asks the secretary to remind the president that she is there. If the secretary checks and conveys that the president will be right with her, the manager will probably remain comfortable until around 1:25. By 1:45, however, she is likely to be quite angry and assume that the president doesn't really care about seeing her.

If the president then has the manager sent in and proceeds directly to the business at hand without offering an explanation, the manager may be irritated, especially if they are a Relater. This may negatively affect the meeting and the relationship. If the president apologizes for being late and shares some inside information with her explanation, the manager is more apt to forgive the boss because, after all, her time is more important.

Time Shows Priority

Whom we spend our time with and what we spend it doing tells people WHO and WHAT we value. If we choose to spend time going to a child's soccer game, rather than working overtime, it is a signal that we value the importance of our children over our work. If we choose to spend time crunching the bottom-line numbers, rather than listening to help solve an employee's problem, it sends a negative message of our priority to the employee. While some demands of our time seem beyond our control, we constantly show everyone around us our likes, dislikes, and priorities by HOW we use our time.

"The Rules" regarding time are simple and well known, although they don't seem to be followed as often as they should be. In order to avoid negative impressions and counter-productive work relationships through your use or abuse of time, work on being punctual. Let others know if you can't meet a time commitment. Don't keep people waiting, but if you do, plan to deal with their feelings of hostility about the wait.

Don't impose unusual schedules that will obviously conflict with personal schedules or holidays; instead do a better job of advanced planning. If you try to fit too many tasks and appointments into the limits of your time, you know that something will fall through the cracks, so plan in advance to avoid over scheduling.

Don't change the time you spend with a person without giving them a reason for the change. Being considerate with our use of time and openly stating the reasons for changes or "rule" violations can go a long way in avoiding misunderstandings and building productive relationships that lead to true authority in your position.

Receive Cooperation From your Co-workers

Increasingly, our ability to accomplish our goals and objectives depends on the cooperation and assistance of our co-workers. This interdependency increases the opportunity for conflict. For example: Accounting needs information from the Sales Department in order to complete financial reports; Sales needs product information from Manufacturing in order to make sales; Manufacturing needs the right parts from Purchasing; Marketing needs information from Customer Service for a new advertising campaign.

Because of interdependency, cooperation among co-workers is extremely important. Organizations are an interrelated web of departments, teams, and individuals and therefore no one can effectively do their job without the input of someone else. When that someone else is late, has a different view of priorities, misunderstands directions, or is playing politics, conflicts are created and cooperation diminishes.

When you listen to the needs of the other person, and sincerely try to help them, they will likely feel good about you. Good feelings about the other person leads to increased trust and credibility, increasing the willingness toward cooperation. In organizations, this generally means a reduction in turnover, more of a commitment to the organization's goals, and increased cooperation among co-workers. Could you benefit from an increase in cooperation from your co-workers?

Space Commands Respect: Good communicators respect, understand, and effectively respect the space of the other person. The payoff of respecting space is more attention, more trust, better communication, and a better chance for productive working relationships.

If someone violates a person's "space" without verbal or nonverbal invitation, it most likely will lead to an increased tension level and a decreased trust level. The relationship often becomes nonproductive, with little or no cooperation. In attempting to build trust, be careful not to offend a person by intruding on their personal space or territory.

You gain cooperation with others when you value the privacy of others and do not make clumsy attempts to invade it. There are detrimental consequences for people who are insensitive to the personal space rules of behavior: an increase in tension, a decrease in credibility, and a reduced chance of gaining commitment or agreement on the subject of the communication. Don't be insensitive to the space of others. Gain their increased cooperation by your sensitivity to this personal and private area of their life.

Earn Support from Upper Management

When you really want upper management to "buy" your ideas and programs, you need to prove your versatility as the leader of your show or event team. Management is not likely to stick their necks out to promote and support your ideas and programs if you do not have the versatility traits to overcome situations and deliver the results expected from your position.

There are five primary versatility traits that will in most cases get your ideas heard, promoted, and supported by upper management. The five versatility traits to cultivate and practice are:

Toughness

Toughness means knowing how to handle the situation in spite of setbacks, roadblocks, or limited resources. Toughness is a measure of how much you want something and how much you're willing and able to overcome obstacles to get there. Toughness has to do with your emotional strength. For instance, how many cold calls can you make while being rejected each and every time? What is your breaking or quitting point?

Toughness is an uncommon but valuable ability. It relates well to other traits like self control and determination. Versatility traits build on flexible attitudes and toughness compels you to be flexible in many situations. Having a sense of confidence in your abilities and maintaining a positive expectation toward people and situations lays the foundation for toughness.

Foresight

The next versatility trait you want to practice is Foresight. Someone who has the power to imagine, to be creative, to deliver alternatives in a clear way that others can understand will have more influence than someone who can't.

Foresight is your clear, distinct picture of a point in the future. Foresight provides a way for people to develop goals and decide the action plans to meet them. With change happening at a rapid rate in the "information age," it has become necessary to envision the way we need things to be in the future. Without foresight, we get run over by the pace of our daily lives and overwhelmed by the feeling of being out of control.

How would you go about developing foresight that would be attractive to other people? Here's the starting point: Use many "what-if" questions in your thinking. "What-if" questions get your imagination and thinking going. One thing that all creative thinkers know is that you should not limit your foresight. Don't assume any rules or limitations. Don't say: "What if we could plan and implement this event with only four people?" and then immediately stop yourself by saying: "No, that will never work." You only limit your ability to look past the current situation.

Foresight is used for many reasons: to make money, to end a problem, to improve a situation, to create an alternative, to have more fun. Some people have foresight where other people see only problems or nothing at all. Is the glass half full, half empty, or running over in the way you look at life? The way you think will certainly prosper or limit you in your efforts to succeed with the direction of upper management.

Awareness

The next trait we'll consider is important to creating foresight. This trait is Awareness and is defined as a constant understanding of the happenings in your environment. It can be as simple as noticing when someone is getting bored, to sensing that now is not the right time to present your ideas. Awareness knows when to act and when not to act.

Awareness is also the ability to disassemble a problem and break it down into its essential components. When you break down the problem, you learn about what is really happening. The insight of awareness provides the basis for seeing solutions that will truly work better.

Awareness means you're open to outside influences redirecting your attention or, if the sensory inputs are subtler, entering your intuition. It means you are open to more information coming in through your eyes and ears, through your sense of touch and through what's known as your kinesthetic sense. That means how your muscles and the organs of your body react. Our bodies can tell us about how other people are feeling if we're aware enough. Being aware of others allows you access to the other person's feelings, and sometimes those feelings are mirrored in your own body – feelings such as fear, sadness and discomfort.

In order to be aware, we need to empty ourselves of distractions and common ways of seeing things. When we use our senses to take in all we can about other people, we can accurately adjust our behavior to the needs of others. When we are aware to others' situations, we can exercise that power of foresight to make positive changes for others and ourselves.

Comprehension

The fourth versatility trait is comprehension. Comprehension goes beyond having a specific expertise. It means being knowledgeable and skillful in your field. But it also means possessing a problem-solving ability that goes beyond your own specialty. When you are able to solve problems in areas beyond your immediate responsibility, you demonstrate an increased value to the company.

If you don't know the answer, or how to fix the problem, comprehension will let you find someone who does. Comprehension means having a "can-do" attitude and following through until you get answers or results.

Exhibiting comprehension in your job, or knowing how to get something done, is communicated to others in a variety of ways. There's the obvious level of being able to do what you say you can do. But comprehension can also be communicated subtly.

Your nonverbal actions – how you look, the sound of your voice – go a long way toward conveying comprehension and confidence. Comprehension is also shown in the style of behavior you choose – whether you come across as a very casual person, or as someone who's a professional and takes life seriously. The style of behavior you <u>choose</u> is important to know because you do have a choice. You are not "born that way."

You can choose to behave in a way that shows comprehension, or you can choose to undercut what skills you do have by looking and acting as if you're not sure of yourself. Upper management always looks to promote and support employees with a wide range of comprehension, and the personal confidence to go with it.

Your ability to gain influence with upper management is dependent on how they <u>see</u> you. Management may hear about you, and use outside input to make an initial impression. But they judge you to be trustworthy and able to manage the tasks you claim you can by what they see you do. You'll go a long way toward gaining trust and support of upper management when you're able to show them your overall comprehension by your actions.

Self-Correction

The fifth versatility trait is Self-Correction. Self-correction is the ability to observe your need for change, the willingness to implement the change, and the comprehension to impartially evaluate your outcomes. It means you are not afraid of feedback and use feedback as motivation to improve yourself. You don't feel the constant need to be right. Instead, you see when you've developed a non-productive pattern in your behavior and say: "I know this approach isn't working, I need to try something different."

Self-correction is based on <u>negative feedback</u>. When things are going well, we generally don't think about changing anything. It's only when something goes wrong, or we recognize the potential for it going wrong, that we decide to make corrections. Negative feedback is based on soliciting and receiving unfavorable information from outside sources. A very simple example is when you receive an average or below-par yearly evaluation from your boss. Evaluations usually have some good points, and are generally on the positive side for good employees. But if there were instances of conduct or performance flaws listed on the report, you'd be thinking about them and how to correct the flaws. That's the principle of negative feedback.

When you possess the trait of self-correction, sometimes called "course-correction," you are willing and able to learn from your mistakes. You seek the path of improvement and do not avoid it. You also get better and better at spotting the need for change in yourself and others before disaster strikes. This ability of preventative correction is extremely valuable to an employer. This isn't to say that you have to be the company watchdog; that will certainly erode your ability to gain cooperation from anyone. Instead, you get to problems early while they are small. It is being able to monitor symptoms of problems before they turn into serious situations.

Earn the Respect of Your Peers

Your voice, handshake, body posture, clothes, and grooming make a tremendous difference in the reception you receive from other people. First impressions do count, and you are measured for success and respect in the blink of an eye. Just take a look at how you judge another person when you first meet them. The first thing you see is their dress, and you have an immediate opinion of them based on what you see. People review you the same way. If you do not present an appropriate image to create a positive impression with other people, those impressions will count against you. Do the best you can to make great impressions.

Your voice is also a tool in your means to earn respect from your peers. How you speak, the tone, the pace, and the caliber of the words you use tell others of your skills and self-confidence. Make sure that you speak clearly and with enough volume to be easily understood. If you tend to speak softly, try your best to speak louder in a way that projects greater authority. To develop this skill, speak about things you know very well. You will find it easier to have confidence and project yourself when you have a passion and understanding of the subject manner.

Handshakes are also very important. You need to extend your hand warmly to the other person, and be able to get a deep, firm grip to their hand. Notice I said firm, but not crushing. There is a difference. However, going deep into the other person's hand is important as it signals a willingness to get to know them, as well as a feeling of confidence in yourself. A handshake that is weak, especially one that only allows for a grip of the other person's fingers, shows a degree of fear and uncertainty. If you are a person who naturally dislikes giving handshakes and therefore applies the minimum effort and grip, do your best to change to the deep and firm grip. Practice with a close friend if need be, but improve your handshake. It is a standard greeting in American business, and increasingly used in the worldwide market as borders and cultural boundaries disappear.

Your body posture displays your self-confidence and general attitude about yourself from a great distance. When you look at a successful person in your company, more than likely you will see that they carry themselves in a way that projects a strong, confident self-image. The head is held high, the shoulders are back, they take longer strides, and they smile! (Don't forget the smile. You don't have to be stern in your facial appearance to gain respect. Look warm.) If you can, have someone videotape you walking down a hallway, and videotape you standing in a show booth and sitting at your desk. Then watch the tape of yourself. See if you can improve your posture or body position in a way that shows confidence and authority. You will also find that the smile comes easier when you project a strong posture.

It has long been said, "clothing makes the man." In today's workplace, clothing also makes the woman, and the way you dress is almost always the first and last item on the list of how other people view you, and the level of respect they give to you. Just think of the most respected people in your company, and compare them with the least successful, or at a minimum, the least respected. Is there a difference, a *dramatic* difference, in how they present themselves each day in their attire?

Although clothing is not the only consideration in earning the respect of your peers, it is indeed a powerful image-maker. Through tasteful and professional dress, you command more respect from others and receive positive responses to your personality. Respect and positive response give you an increased chance of success with other people.

Most organizations have their own cultural dress codes that often vary by department and status in the organization. If you're a middle manager, you may walk a clothing tightrope trying to project an aura of authority and success in order to move up in the hierarchy while not putting too much distance between you and your employees. Not easy situations to solve, but if you are in doubt about the level of dress as a middle manager, always go toward the higher-end. Dressing down does not always send the right message. Let them see you dressed well while at the same time being willing to reach down and help a colleague or subordinate. You earn greater respect from your peers by your willingness to help and not step on them.

Relatively speaking, men have the easier road in earning respect through dress. Not as many choices between shirts, suits, ties, or collarless attire. On the other hand, women have the complication of trying to establish the right image without losing their feminine identity. Although the choices of dress for women are many and this sounds like a tough order to dress for success, know that it can be done.

To start your respect-earning process, think through the image that you want to project within the cultural environment of your organization. If you want to rise in the organization, there's no point in wearing expensive suits if the CEO is a casual, shirtsleeve type. That would make you stand out among your peers, but would be a subtle sign of disrespect to your boss. Instead, if you want to project authority while earning respect, dress in a conservative manner and at a fashion slightly higher than the people you serve.

If your height, weight, or age is creating an emotional problem or an image problem for you, use clothing to diminish those problems. For instance, a tall person might soften the impact of their height by wearing soft colors and textures while avoiding dark, heavy, overpowering clothing. Make the appearance of being more inviting and less intimidating. Dark colors intimidate while softer colors are warm and welcoming.

Short people create more visual impact by doing the opposite. They might want to wear more authoritative clothing, such as dark suits, sweaters, solid color shirts with matching color ties, and the long, narrow Italian-style shoes that help lengthen the body parts. If you are a woman, dark-colored, tailored suits and plain, high-quality blouses can help your situation. If you want to wear jewelry, keep it simple and tasteful. Silver or pewter colors work well. Try to avoid much gold or flashy jewelry. Focus the attention on your personality and the command of your presence, not distract with an aspect of your attire.

Heavy people can wear dark suits and loose-fitting outer clothing to de-emphasize their weight, whereas thin people can wear lighter shades of clothing to make them look a bit heavier.

Young people, who may need to project more power and authority, can follow the same guidelines as those recommended for shorter people. Project an image of greater power with the darker colors.

Older people, whose age already carries power and authority, can follow the same advice as that recommended for taller people.

Finally, grooming carries the last details of your "total package" that helps or hinders your ability to earn respect from your peers. If you are a younger man, closely trimmed facial hair will add a few years to your appearance, but keep all facial hair well groomed as well as your hair. Avoid long haircuts and beards, and set yourself on a regular schedule to get haircuts and trims. Make sure you get a fresh haircut and trim before attending shows, important meetings, and customer events. If you still wear facial hair, you can project a younger appearance by being clean-shaven. If you choose to keep facial hair, groom close to avoid a sloppy appearance.

For a younger woman, a shorter-length haircut will give the appearance of maturity that translates into greater respect from peers. For an older woman, you are almost expected to have a shorter haircut or risk losing respect. If your hair is longer and you are older, consider wearing it up or tied back in some way.

Normally, your style of dress projects either a conservative, authoritative, and successful image, or a carefree, less motivated image. To earn respect and increase your upward mobility, take a good look to those who are in front of you, and do your best to dress accordingly. If you are currently a manager, an upgraded image through conservative and authoritative dress will prompt your employees to take you more seriously.

Be Recognized in Your Corporate Family

The easiest way to be recognized in your corporate family is based on your ability to be flexible. Flexibility and the ability to get along with others in situations is an attribute that many employers covet in their key people. Most positions in the trade show sector of a company involve many different roles and have some dealings with almost all of the functional areas of a company. In order to relate to all the types of people in all the situations you would encounter as a Show Manager or Events Coordinator, you need to be flexible.

There are definite traits that are inherent in a truly flexible person in an organization. Let's focus on five positive traits for flexibility, the ones you want to develop and refine. They are:

1. Confidence

2. Tolerance

3. Empathy

4. Positiveness

5. Respect

Confidence

Having confidence means you believe in yourself and you trust your own judgment and abilities. In his many books on self-esteem, Dr. Nathaniel Branden defines confidence as knowing that you have the ability and knowledge to succeed in whatever you do.

When you are confident in yourself, you are energized to make choices that satisfy your needs, help others, and chart the course for your life. Having confidence in specific situations, such as gaining a relationship or influence with someone, would flow from an overall self-confidence about your ability to meet the other person on equal ground.

Please understand that even the most confident person is going to get some negative feedback once in a while. But the confident person doesn't let it diminish his or her self-esteem. Confidence in you is built up or torn down over time, not overnight. You can fake confidence, and you may need to at first, but real self-confidence comes from a history of small victories and accomplishments that add up to a sense that you can handle yourself well in most every situation. It is built almost through a series of life exercises.

We suggest you take an inventory of both the major and minor accomplishments you've achieved over the past few years. Have you built anything that is still standing? What about those kids you're raising? Have you grown both professionally, personally, and spiritually?

Don't be modest. Tell the truth about how hard you worked and note the sacrifices you've made. If you can't think of any, then begin by congratulating yourself for living as long as you have, and/or doing the best you can do in your job. Sheer survival is an accomplishment these days!

It pays to take the time to know your strengths, see them in action, and appreciate them. Your strengths and accomplishments are the attributes that are unique about you. Build your confidence by identifying the talents and skills you bring to an organization or project that no one else has.

Tolerance

Flexibility trait number two is tolerance. Tolerance means you're open to accepting opinions and practices that are different from your own. Tolerant people get the attention of a diverse audience.

We all grow up with people who are different from us. How we deal with those people at an early age gives us the ability to translate our flexibility into tolerance as adults. It does not mean that you always agree or approve of the other person, but you do your best to see the world from their eyes, and find ways to work with them, rather than against them. But unfortunately we don't all start out with a high degree of tolerance. Some of us have to learn tolerance and grow our skills in this area.

Remember that true flexibility means that you're willing to adapt your behavior. You're less likely to do that with an intolerant attitude toward the other person. Intolerance is a double-edged sword. It may keep those people you don't like at a distance. But it isolates you within your group. In order to gain a high degree of recognition in your corporate family, your flexibility trait of tolerance of the views and backgrounds of others will serve you well.

Empathy

Empathy is the third positive flexibility trait. The root of the word empathy is PATHOS – the Greek word for feeling. Sympathy means acknowledging the feelings of someone else as in "I sympathize with you." Empathy is different. Empathy is a term for a deeper feeling that means, "I feel what you feel. I can put myself in your shoes." Sympathy results in kindness and sometimes pity. Empathy results in actually feeling the pain, or the joy, of the other person.

You can see how the willingness to be flexible comes more easily when you can put yourself in the other person's shoes. Empathy is a valuable trait to possess, and is a key skill taught in negotiating. Human beings have a deep need for their feelings to be recognized. Knowing and actually feeling empathy can help in a difficult negotiation by creating the climate for agreement.

William Ury in his book _Getting Past No_ counsels that it's important to acknowledge both the actual point and the feelings of the other person. He uses the example of an employee approaching a boss.

The employee says: "I just found out Regina makes $5000 more a year than I do for the same job." Trying to explain why Regina makes more money, even if the reason is a good one, only makes the employee angrier. Instead, you must acknowledge the fact and their feelings before you discuss the matter. You say: "You think we're taking advantage of you and you're angry. I can understand that. I'd probably feel the same way if I were you."

That isn't what an angry person expects. By acknowledging the employee's feelings, you've helped them calm down. His next statement might be: "Well, why shouldn't I make as much as Regina does?" That shows he's ready to hear your explanation.

The feeling of empathy is much easier to come by when you care about the other person and take the time to feel what they're feeling. In the worlds of business, politics, or the professions, that feeling of empathy may not come as easily because you don't have the time and bandwidth to be empathic with all your people's problems. However, the best managers, the ones most recognized by their employees and peers, almost always have this trait in abundance.

Please use caution when practicing empathy. You might be concerned that expressing a caring approach toward another person will result in the other person manipulating you. They won't manipulate you if you don't give up your own needs or point of view. Having empathy simply means that you're able to step into the shoes of another and acknowledge their feelings.

Having the ability of empathy is an asset. You can always wear your own shoes. Why not wear the shoes of the other person and see the improvement in the responses you receive?

Positiveness

The next trait is Positiveness. It means maintaining a state of positive expectations about people and situations, including a positive state of energy in your thoughts and emotions. Dr. Norman Vincent Peale's book, _The Power of Positive Thinking_, was published many years ago. The book is a foundational text and continues to sell well because it contains the universal truth that our attitudes and thoughts shape our lives on a daily basis.

Having a positive attitude isn't something you just tack on to your old personality. Positiveness comes from deep within you and is built on a strong, often spiritual foundation. Positiveness is having an upbeat, confident life philosophy exhibited through your strengths.

People with lasting positiveness surround themselves with other sources of positiveness.

Many of us haven't taken the time to consider our own life philosophy. If you haven't, it doesn't mean you don't have one. You're just operating from it unconsciously. By life philosophy, we mean your potential and willingness to make a contribution to society, and still have a good time getting there. Many positive people say: I'm here to serve God through being of service to my fellow human beings. Another philosophy might be: I'm here to show others that despite physical handicaps, you can lead a productive life and enjoy what you have.

Another aspect of positiveness comes from knowing your strengths. This involves taking a personal inventory of your talents and skills and also what you like to do. Ideally, we'd all like to make a living by spending our time doing what we love.

The people who come the closest to a deep and lasting positiveness are those who actually take the time to figure out what they love doing, and then take the steps to mold their true love and passion into their ideal life's work.

To maintain your positiveness for a lifetime, you must surround yourself with other people with the same positive energy. Negative people will drain you of your positive energy, so you must avoid them on a constant basis. Unfortunately people who are negative by nature often don't want to change; they draw significance and strength from their negativity. However, you don't want to spend time with that crowd.

Occasionally we hear stories of people who struggle against great odds and achieve the nearly impossible. To overcome large odds, you need a positive philosophy to get results, and knowledge of what you can do yourself and what you need from others. Success stories rarely mention the fact that those people always had some other source of positive energy outside themselves that kept them going. Often it is a combination of spiritual strength and strength from other positive people they could rely on for support. Therefore, surround yourself with the kinds of people who exhibit positive traits and avoid the people with the negative traits. These people don't help you recharge, they drain you.

The trait of positiveness is so attractive; other people will be drawn to you. That in turn, will help you to develop the other positive traits of confidence, tolerance and empathy that we've discussed.

Respect for Others

The fifth positive flexibility trait we'll consider is respect for others. This entire book was built around the trait of respect for others through the examples and applications of The Platinum Rule. Again, to emphasize this trait, The Platinum Rule says: "Do unto others as they want to be done unto." The Platinum Rule demonstrates respect for others by helping to avoid the possible conflicts the often-used Golden Rule could unintentionally set up.

When using The Golden Rule and treating others as you want to be treated, you can end up offending others who have different needs, wants and expectations from you. Following the Golden Rule verbatim means treating others from your point of view. That means you naturally tend to speak in the way you are most comfortable listening, or sell the way you like to be sold, or manage the way you like others to direct you.

When you treat people as you seek to be treated, it can cause tension because the other person may not appreciate or like your way of doing things. That brings us to the second reason the Golden Rule can actually damage relationships. It implies that all people wanted to be treated the same when our preferences are not all alike. So the application of this principle varies from one individual to the next based on their personality differences and behavioral styles.

That's why The Platinum Rule comes in handy. It says: "Treat others the way they want to be treated." By using the word "platinum" we don't mean to imply that this rule is <u>better</u>. We simply want to capture the true spirit or actual intention of the Golden Rule and be able to respond appropriately to the other person's needs. Respecting others means learning to sometimes treat different people differently, according to their needs, not ours. This leads to greater respect for the other person through your deference to their true needs.

Summary: Considering the five positive traits of flexibility as discussed in this section, know that they contribute to the overall quality of your life experience. These traits give us the ability to be consistent in our attitude toward ourselves, and our approach to others. We need to be consistent in our dealings with others, seven days a week, as well as having a keen insight into our actions and ourselves.

How much better would you feel if you were more confident about yourself? More tolerant of others? If you had more empathy for their pain? If you viewed other people in the positive rather than the negative? And if your respect for others extended to caring about the way you treat them? Having positive traits puts you strongly in the position of being willing to adapt your behavior to meet the needs of others while taking you away from feeling like an orphan in your corporate family.

THE END OF THIS BOOK, A NEW BEGINNING

It has taken many pages and many hours to move past the story of John and his first trade show, given at the beginning of this book. Since we are near the end of the book and have learned many lessons, let us see the difference in approach and results John realizes as a trained Platinum Rule trade show professional.

The Tale of Your Next Trade Show

John is a Sales Rep for a major press manufacturer, working his first trade show. John is excited; he loves people, and grew up with a father who was a press operator. He is confident that he can learn as much as he can about the people he meets at the show, because he recently was a graduate of Platinum Rule training.

He knows the information he learns about these new people will help them better understand him as a person, and then will allow them to listen and learn about the value of his presses. He knows this is the sure way to make lots of money because for years his friends always said he had a great ability as a listener. He is eager to start meeting new friends and begin long-term relationships.

"New School Booth work: The "Ask and Listen" Approach

A man in his early 40s enters the booth and approaches a 50-ton press. John walks up, introduces himself and starts asking the prospect about what brought him to the show. He remembers his Platinum Rule training and looks to judge the pace of the prospect's response, and the directness of his approach. The prospect states quickly that he came to the show to see some of his friends and suppliers, then comments about the press's sleek European design, how fast it runs, and how impressive it will look sitting in the his machine shop.

The prospect flips through some papers he brought in with him. He quickly asks John if the press comes with installation, and then asks a question about the process monitor for part quality and safety. John answers his question and enthusiastically mentions that a major supplier to Ford just bought the very same model.

The prospect asks if the press "really cranks out the parts," and then without waiting for the answer suggests how happy his operators will be to run the new touch screen controller on the press. The prospect quickly folds his papers, thanks John for his time, tells him to come by the machine shop some time, and leaves... all in less than three minutes.

John knows that the meeting with the prospect revealed that his subject was a Socializer, and he notes the likely behavioral style on his prospect booth card. He also notes that the prospect was enthused with the design, and really liked the idea that other major suppliers to Ford made the same purchase. He asks his sales manager if he may schedule a "fast track" personalized marketing campaign to send the prospect four items of interest in the press in the next three weeks. He also asks if Business Development would enter the prospect into the Cyrano web-based lead development system at the show.

The manager agrees and before the prospect reaches the end of the aisle, he is sent an email that has a picture of the press at John's booth, and thanks him for stopping by. In two more minutes, the Lead Development Coordinator working in the booth schedules 12 different personalized marketing touches to be mailed and emailed to the prospect in the next six months.

All the touches discuss the fact that many major suppliers use this press, and include testimonials from operators about the ease and fun of running the press. Another prospect identified, qualified, and started in their personal follow-up program. John then looks to the aisle for the next prospect.

If at First You Succeed, Do it again...

Two young engineers walk over and look at the same press. John introduces himself and learns they have an appointment scheduled from their pre-show marketing campaign. Their purpose is to discuss the press and learn about its construction and all its safety features. The meeting was scheduled for Tim their Technical Service Rep. John asks if he can contribute to the meeting and they agree. John quickly identifies one of the engineers as a Director, and the second as a Thinker.

To address both of their behavioral styles, John assures them that this press is a very efficient model, with the lowest set-up times for its class and the greatest profit per part. Then the Thinker asks about the parts per minute rating and the other remarks that it looks kind of "light-duty," unable to produce their volumes profitably. Tim the Tech Rep quickly gives the exceptional torque and tonnage ratings to the Thinker, and tells the Director that "European transfer presses" produce the greatest output efficiency and bottom-line profits of any press in its class.

They tell John they were originally "just looking" but after learning these new details would like to discuss the specifics of a project they are quoting for Chrysler. The Thinker asks Tim for more details and prints on the tool layouts, and the Director asks Tim about the fastest availability and any incentives for buying a press at the show.

After the prospects leave, John sits down and makes notes on his booth card, noting the name and style of the Thinker and Director, and how one was interested in the details of the press, and the other was interested in the profit per part capability. He then hands the two prospect booth cards to the Lead Development Coordinator who sends the same email picturing the press at their booth, and an eight-touch marketing campaign to the Director, stressing profits and technical advantage of the transfer press, and the construction, tool and electrical controls tech advantages to the Thinker.

All these follow-up campaigns are scheduled in the Cyrano System from an automated burst campaign that they set up the month before the show. In less than five minutes, both prospects are scheduled to receive exactly what they want, when they want it. John can now forget about that lead (although he has visions of the commission check), and move toward listening to the needs and situations of the next prospects to visit their booth.

Tim scratches his head and wonders why they did not learn "this Platinum Rule stuff" earlier in their careers. He now knows he has a skill that he will carry into any field because he knows how to relate to the style of any prospect or customer he encounters, helping make them comfortable quickly and want to work with him. He now realizes how fun practicing his Platinum Rule skills is, and no longer worries about how he will pay his bills.

What did John do right? A *Platinum Rule* Advisor would say, "Almost everything." He quickly identified the style of each person he met, did not try to sell anything before he knew what their style was, and therefore what they most likely wanted. He asked questions about what his prospects wanted and why they came to the show, and found out the criteria each customer was using to make their purchasing decisions.

We know that John effectively used two major Platinum Points:

One: John understood his own selling style and how to **adapt** to the needs of each prospect. He fit each prospect into the sales style required to make each prospect first comfortable with him, and then their products. Each was used to identify the prospect's true needs.

Two: John understood the basic **process** of booth "sales"; i.e. to gather as much qualifying information about the prospect to jump-start the all-important follow-up process. In other words, he listened instead of talked, noted their styles and preferences, took into account their pace, and immediately scheduled an automated, personalized marketing follow-up for each prospect and customer. Different in their timeframes and key message points.

The difference in the trade show as explained above is that the booth staff understood their roles in the play, and played their parts flawlessly. They knew the goals and outcomes for the show going in, and did not try to pressure anyone into a sale at the show. They knew that building the trust and relationship first would lead to a greater likelihood of legitimate sales opportunities and long-term relationships. They also knew that the pressure to sell at the show is off, that time and gentle pressure will convert a prospect that looks like a lump of coal eventually into a diamond.

Would you like your trade shows and booth staff to look like John and Tim? What do you need to do to get your program started in that direction?

Start Now and Take Ownership of Your Destiny

Imagine what would have happened if you had successfully applied the principles and practices of *The Platinum Rule For Trade Show Mastery* ten years ago... or just five years ago? Well, tens of thousands of people like you have already used Platinum Rule principles and experienced dramatic increases in sales volumes, more satisfaction in their dealings with customers and co-workers (family and friends, also!), and greater awareness of their own strengths and weaknesses.

Platinum Rule practitioners report that they no longer feel like a "salesperson." Instead, they feel, behave, and are treated like a trusted advisor. They have an increased ability to help people find solutions to their problems and are more adept at identifying new opportunities to help other people.

For you to also share in the pleasure from experiencing these benefits, we encourage you to get started practicing your behavior identification skills today, before you do anything else. First, think about the goals you want to accomplish in the next year... the next month... the next week... and, finally, by the end of today! Develop a plan to meet those goals using **The Platinum Rule** and the other principles that make up *The Platinum Rule for Trade Show Mastery.*

Accept the Challenge

This first step requires your *personal commitment* to this challenge and *belief* in the Platinum Rule principles. Your success is increased with other people when you can learn to put the Platinum rules to work for you. Of course, any skill takes practice, and you cannot realistically expect to put all of them into immediate effect. However, the minute you start to treat people they way *they* want to be treated, you will start to see immediate results. We encourage you to accept this opportunity to strengthen your personal selling abilities!

Develop a Plan

Once you have accepted the challenge, you need a plan to incorporate these techniques into your life. Although we have provided you with an extremely simple, effective method of identifying behavior styles, it does take a plan to work these skills into your trade shows, events, career, family, and life. Like anything worth learning, the Platinum Rule skills take ongoing practice to master.

Deliver the Goods

Once you have your plan, and "why" you want to be a practitioner of The Platinum Rule in your trade shows and events, you have to get out there and deliver the goods! Be the company that has people who are "different," and thereby considered better by your customers. People will not immediately understand how you are different, and they might not care, but the fact that you have a personal interest and a natural bond with your prospects and customers will carry you past others who are just out to force a sale.

You have to practice The Platinum Rule to be personally effective, so get out and deliver the goods!

Report Back To Us!

We always welcome your feedback on the content and life-changing effects of this book. In addition, if you would like to have your stories considered for inclusion in future *Platinum Rule* books, then contact us through our website at www.platinumrulegroup.com You can also opt-in to our marketing newsletter that will send you the tips and information you need based on your style and requests. All you have to do is click on the *"One-to-one from A-Z"* button and submit your information. We will send you the information you want, when you want it.

We welcome you to share what works, and what does not work, as your experiences will certainly help others by improving future editions of this book.

We thank you for your interest, desire, and commitment to making The Platinum Rule a way of life for your trade show and exhibit business, and look forward to seeing people helping each other and building long-term, profitable relationships with a Platinum Revolution in the events industry.

Our hope is that with your belief in these teachings and massive action on your parts, this book is the beginning of a great renaissance in real, meaningful, truly personal communications between exhibitors, attendees, co-workers, and families.

ABOUT THE AUTHORS

Tony Alessandra, PhD, CSP, CPAE
Building Customers, Relationships, and the Bottom Line

Dr. Tony Alessandra helps companies achieve market dominance through specific strategies designed to outmarket, outsell, and outservice the competition.

Dr. Alessandra has a street-wise, college-smart perspective on business, having realized success as former a graduate professor of marketing, entrepreneur, business author and keynote speaker. He earned his **BBA**, **MBA** and **PhD**, all in Marketing, from the University of Notre Dame, the University of Connecticut, and Georgia State University, respectively.

Dr. Tony Alessandra is president of **AssessmentBusinessCenter. com**, a company that offers online 360° assessments; Chairman of **BrainX.com**, a company that created the first Online Learning Mastery System™; and is the founding partner of **Platinum Rule Group (www. PlatinumRuleGroup.com)**, a company that provides corporate training, one-to-one marketing technology and consulting based on *The Platinum Rule*®.

Dr. Alessandra is a widely published author with 15 books translated into 17 foreign languages, including *The Platinum Rule for Sales Mastery, The Platinum Rule for Small Business Mastery, The Platinum Rule*, *Charisma, Collaborative Selling*, and *Communicating at Work*. He is featured in over 50 audio/video programs and films, including *Relationship Strategies, The Dynamics of Effective Listening*, and *Non-Manipulative Selling*.

Dr. Alessandra's television program, "People I.Q." is currently aired on TSTN – The Success Training Network.

Recognized by *Meetings & Conventions Magazine* as "one of America's most electrifying speakers," Dr. Alessandra was inducted into the Speakers Hall of Fame in 1985, and is a member of the Speakers Roundtable, a group of 20 of the world's top professional speakers.

You may reach Dr. Alessandra at: TA@Alessandra.com or calling his office: **(702) 567-9965**

Steve Underation, MBA, CTSM
Converting Trade Show Leads into Long-Term Customers

Steve Underation is a trade show Lead Conversion Specialist, Speaker, and a Coach to profit-minded exhibitors. As Partner of Trade Show Profit Systems, his purpose is to propel companies to dramatic increases in sales, new customers, and profits from their leads.

Steve's customized follow-up systems are the reasons why leads do not disappear into "black holes," but develop customers and sales months and years after the show.

Steve's expertise of transforming trade shows from expenses to profit centers was gained through years of working all sides of the trade show aisle; from exhibitor, to sales rep., to attendee. With 17 years of hands-on experience competing as a high-dollar, technical-based sales rep. for 23 national and international companies, Steve earned ground-level experience with sales reps. and solutions-based results with top management.

Steve is a Certified Trade Show Marketer (CTSM) through Northern Illinois University. He completed his MBA in Marketing through The University of Akron and is an annual guest speaker at the nation's largest trade shows industry conference, The Exhibitor Show. He is the author of *Keep Your Best Leads Out of the Trash and Convert Them to Customers* and the short course *14 Steps to Improve Trade Show Profitability.*

You may learn how Steve can help you keep your best leads out of the trash and convert them to customers by visiting www.TradeShowProfitSystems.com, by contacting Steve's office at 330-753-1616, or by email at Help@TradeShowProfitSystems.com

Scott M. Zimmerman
Transforming Business and Personal Lives with The Platinum Rule

Scott Zimmerman is President of **The Cyrano Group**, and Managing Partner of Platinum Rule Group, companies that provide Platinum Rule® training, communications technologies and sales growth consulting.

In 1991, Zimmerman founded Zimmer Graphics, a full-service marketing/communications firm. He has helped hundreds of companies with positioning, copy writing, graphic design, advertising, promotions, printing and web development.

In 2001, Zimmerman revolutionized business-to-business marketing by unveiling the world's first web-based, fully automated, one-to-one communications system. **The Cyrano Marketing System™** (patents pending) sends customized emails, literature, letters and gifts that match every contact's behavioral style, preferences, interests and critical timing points throughout the relationship cycle. Cyrano builds a real-time, relational database, performs most of the relationship-building work for rainmakers and/or salespeople and is accessible from anywhere in the world.

Today, Zimmerman (and his firm) works with clients who desire to systematize every aspect of their business growth functions: lead acquisition, lead conversion, customer loyalty, and referral programs.

Zimmerman and Alessandra are founders and partners of **Platinum Rule Group,** which was formed to make the philosophy of *"Do Unto Others as **They** Want Done Unto **Them**!"* a common practice throughout the world.

Through books, audio/video programs, speeches, assessments and corporate training, we strive to improve our world by teaching The Platinum Rule®.

In addition to this book, Zimmerman and Alessandra have co-authored *The Platinum Rule for Sales Mastery* and *The Platinum Rule for Small Business Mastery.*

Scott serves as an entrepreneur, author, speaker, trainer and consultant. He may be reached by calling 1-330-848-0444 or via email: Scott@ TheCyranoGroup.com or Scott@PlatinumRuleGroup.com. Scott is the author of The Platinum Rule for Sales Mastery.

CONTRIBUTORS
AND RESOURCES

Joel Bauer
Bauer and Associates
Trade Show Crowds Guaranteed
9909 Topanga Canyon Blvd #202
Chatsworth, CA. 91311
818-882-4949
www.infotainer.com

Exhibitor Magazine Group
Exhibitor Magazine and Event Magazine Publishers
Exhibitor Show and Conference Organizers
206 South Broadway
Suite 745
Rochester, MN 55904
507-289-6556
www.exhibitorshow.com

Michael LaRocca

d/b/a Calico Consulting

Proofreader, Editor, Author

Chiang Mai, Thailand

larocca.michael@gmail.com

www.chinarice.org

Doug MacLean

MacLean Marketing

Trade Show Staff Training, Consulting, Performance Improvement

tradeshowexpert@gmail.com

Steve Miller

The Adventure LLC

Trade Show Speaker, Consultant and Author

32706 - 39th Ave. SW

Federal Way, WA 98023

(253) 874-9665

theadventure@theadventure.com

Diane Silberstein, CMP

Global Connections Marketing Solutions, LLC

National and International Corporate Event Specialist

2405 Macy Drive

Roswell, Georgia 30076

770-645-9290

info@gci-us.com

Ruth Stevens

eMarketing Strategy

Author, Speaker, Direct Marketing Specialist

155 East 34th St., New York, NY, 10016

212-679-6486

ruth@ruthstevens.com

Trade Show Exhibitors Association (TSEA)

TSEA Exhibitor Show and Conference

McCormick Place

2301 South Lake Shore Drive

Suite 1005

Chicago, Illinois 60616

312-842-8732

www.tsea.org

Printed in the USA
CPSIA information can be obtained
at www.ICGtesting.com
JSHW081306291123
52947JS00001B/3